MOTHERING AND FATHERING

The Gender Differences in Child Rearing

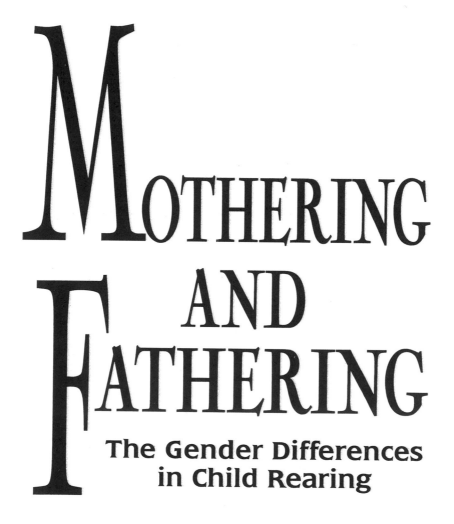

MOTHERING AND FATHERING

The Gender Differences in Child Rearing

TINE THEVENIN

AVERY PUBLISHING GROUP INC.
Garden City Park, New York

Cover designers: Rudy Shur and Ann Vestal
Cover photo supply house: The Stock Market
Cover photographers: Michael A. Keller (top) and Paul Barton
Editor: Amy C. Tecklenburg
Typesetter: Bonnie Freid
Printer: Paragon Press, Honesdale, PA

Also by Tine Thevenin:

The Family Bed: An Age-Old Concept in Child Rearing
Luck Is Not a Butterfly

Library of Congress Cataloging-in-Publication Data

Thevenin, Tine.
    Mothering and fathering : the gender differences in child rearing
/ Tine Thevenin.
      p. cm.
    Includes bibliographical references and index.
    ISBN 0-89529-569-5
    1. Child rearing. 2. Parenting. 3. Sex role. I. Title.
HQ769.T4663 1993
649'.1—dc20   93-13760
                                        CIP

Printed in the United States of America.

10 9 8 7 6 5 4 3

Contents

This book is written for my two lovely daughters, Yvonne and Michelle. This book is dedicated, however, to my wonderful husband Dag Knudsen, whose love and encouragement forever surround me.

CREDITS

The excerpts on pages 25, 31, and 35 are from *Sex and Fantasy* by Robert May. Reprinted by permission of W.W. Norton & Company.

The excerpts on pages 28, 56, 93, 123, and 142 are from *He and She* by Cris Evatt. Reprinted by permission of Conari Press.

The excerpts on pages 34, 67, and 69 are from *Brain Sex*, copyright © 1991 by Anne Moir and David Jessel. Reprinted by permission of Carol Publishing Group.

The excerpts on pages 34, 152, and 156 are from *In Defense of the Family* by Rita Kramer, published by HarperCollins Publishers. Copyright © 1983 by Basic Books, Inc.

The excerpts on pages 90, 92, and 102 are from *Everyday Parenting* by Robin Goldstein. Reprinted by permission of Penguin USA.

The excerpt on pages 96–97 is from *Women as Mothers,* copyright © 1978 by Sheila Kitzinger. Reprinted by permission of Random House, Inc.

The excerpts on page 110 are from *Flow* by Mihaly Csikszentmihalyi, published by HarperCollins Publishers. Copyright © 1990 by Mihaly Csikszentmihalyi.

The excerpts on pages 115–116 are from "SIDS Research" by James McKenna. Excerpted with permission from *Mothering*, Vol. 62. All rights reserved.

The excerpts on pages 129, 159, and 160 are from *On Becoming a Family* by T. Berry Brazelton. Reprinted by permission of Bantam, Doubleday, Dell Publishing Group, Inc.

The excerpt on page 135 is from *The Continuum Concept,* © 1985 by Jean Liedloff. Reprinted by permission of Addison-Wesley Publishing Co., Inc.

The excerpts on pages 138, 140, and 149 are from *Iron John*, © 1990 by Robert Bly. Reprinted with permission of Addison-Wesley Publishing Company, Inc.

The excerpt on page 144 is from *The Road Less Traveled*, by M. Scott Peck, M.D. © 1978 by M. Scott Peck, M.D. Reprinted by permission of Simon & Schuster, Inc.

The excerpt on page 151 is from "A Family Tradition," by Howard Sivertson, in *Once Upon an Isle*. Reprinted by permission of the Wisconsin Folk Museum.

Acknowledgments

Thank you, Edwina Froelich, for your wonderful enthusiasm and your wisdom on issues concerning parenting; Michele Mason, for your exciting support and belief in wholesome parenting; Niles Newton, Ph.D., for your excellent guidance and suggestions and long-time, unwavering support for mothers; Janet Jendron, for your time and suggestions; James McKenna, Ph.D., for your support and the valuable materials you sent me; Lynn Moen, for suggesting a book title for a second time (the first time was your suggestion for the title of my previous book on child rearing, *The Family Bed*); Amy Tecklenburg, my editor at Avery, for your enthusiasm and excellent professional help; and my publisher Rudy Shur, for your suggestions, your support, your great sensitivity to writers, and your genuine interest in doing all you can for your authors.

Foreword

Mothering *and* fathering—the title says it all. Both parents have unique contributions to make in the development of a child. The issue is not whether mothers are better parents than fathers (or vice versa), or whether one gender is more often right or wrong than the other. Mothers and fathers think differently, act differently, and have different views on child rearing. And children thrive on these different approaches. In this book, Tine Thevenin—whose previous book, *The Family Bed*, we grew to love—points out how men and women are biologically and emotionally different, how the different characteristics of the two sexes complement each other, and, most important, how children profit from this. Mothers usually are content to allow children to be dependent, while fathers encourage children to be independent. Herein lies the balance that mothers and fathers bring to child rearing.

Mothers and fathers who read this book will better understand why their mates think and act the way they do.

When a baby cries, the male may slowly walk toward the upset child—only to be outrun by the female, who sprints toward her crying baby and scoops her new little one up within seconds of the opening sound. She is made that way; so is he. Mothers usually rush to comfort crying babies. Fathers allow babies more time to work through the fussiness by themselves. And much of this reaction stems from basic biological differences between the genders. When a baby cries, the blood flow to a mother's breasts increases, and she has a biological urge to comfort her baby. The baby's cry does not trigger such biological changes in the male, even though fathers may love their babies just as much and be equally sensitive to their needs.

Fathers have more than a supporting role to play in baby-tending. They are more than substitute mothers, pinch-hitting while mom is away. This realization is more important in today's society than ever before. If women must share in working to produce income, then men must share in child rearing.

By beautifully portraying the strengths of each gender and valuing them equally, Tine Thevenin has taken on the politically correct realm of the unisex philosophy and exposed its weakness. Hurray for her. We believe that after reading this book, not only will moms and dads be more sensitive parents, they will become more sensitive partners.

Dr. William and Martha Sears
Authors of *The Baby Book*

Preface

Globally and historically, the raising of children has been the domain of women. Books of medical advice on child rearing written by men, on the other hand, began to proliferate in the Western world only in the last 150 years or so. Yet in that comparatively short span of time, we have come to consider men to be the experts on the subject. Meanwhile, a growing body of serious research is beginning to support the idea that men and women are different not only physically, but also emotionally, psychologically, and in myriad other ways. It should come as no surprise, therefore, that men and women differ also in their fundamental beliefs about raising children, although this simple fact has received surprisingly little attention. Since we now face a situation where the primary sources of information about child rearing are male experts, even as increasing amounts of research are becoming available about the essential differences between men and women, I believe we must take a second look at some of the child-rearing advice so widely accepted in our culture today.

This book is designed to create an awareness of why both men and women feel the way they do toward child rearing, and to foster an understanding of why their approaches differ and how each approach has a place in the child-rearing process. It explores the influence of male experts, and especially the origins and consequences of their insistence that babies and young children be taught independence from early childhood on, as well as women's often deeply emotionally driven desire for intimacy with their children, which so often conflicts with the male approach.

This awareness will help both men and women to understand and appreciate each other's emotions and values. It will give men a greater appreciation of maternal feelings and help women understand why the advice of their husbands, male doctors, and child-rearing books written by men so often seems at odds with their own instincts. It will also foster greater awareness of the need for a man's presence in the child-rearing process. In addition, it will help parents understand that there is a difference between nurturing and smothering, as there is between encouraging a child and pushing him beyond his limits.

My goal in writing this book is to give insight into and encourage the acceptance of the mother's perspective; to help eliminate the tension and unhappiness that result when women try to adopt men's emotions and ignore their own, especially when their children are very young; and to bring the importance of the male approach into perspective. Above all, my goal is to create mutual understanding that will benefit children and enhance the child-rearing experience for the whole family.

A Word About Gender

A baby is as likely to be a boy as a girl; however, our language does not provide us with a singular pronoun that includes both genders. To avoid using the awkward "he/she" or the impersonal "it" when referring to babies, while still giving equal time to both sexes, the feminine pronouns "she" and "her" have been used in odd-numbered chapters and the masculine pronouns "he," "him," and "his," have been used in even-numbered chapters. This decision has been made in the interest of simplicity and clarity.

Introduction

Q. Who are the primary caretakers of young children?
A. Women.
Q. Who are the nationally known experts on raising children?
A. Men.

For the first time in recorded history, men are considered the experts in child rearing. An overwhelming number of the books available on the subject have been written by men. This is a situation unique to modern Western society, and its consequences are not always desirable. Women are (as they have always been) the primary caregivers for young children, yet the people giving them advice on what to do are men—even though they have never given birth, breast-fed, or developed a special maternal intimacy with a child.

Men and women are different. More and more research is becoming available on just how they differ—not only physically, but also emotionally, psychologically, and in how they solve problems, react to stress, view relationships, and communicate, with adults as well as with children. Basically, men generally strive for independence, while women generally strive for interdependence. An independent person is one who prefers to "go it alone," to be in control, and who seeks to stay that way. An interdependent person is one who, although capable of being on her own, seeks intimacy and connectedness with others, whether family, friends, or coworkers. (Both of these are different from a dependent person, who has difficulty relying on himself and instead must rely on others to function well.)

Men and women differ in their ideas about raising children because of these underlying gender differences. Women tend to be *nurturers*, seeking to connect, be intimate with, and respond to their children. Men tend to be what I call *encouragers*, stressing the development of children's independence.

When men give women advice on how to rear children, they often, in effect, urge mothers to adopt the feelings and reactions of men. This can lead to misunderstandings, conflict, and heartache.

For example:

- A baby is put in his crib for the night but begins to cry. His mother wants to pick him up and rock him, but she knows that many (male) experts say, "It's good for him to learn to go to sleep by himself."

- A nineteen-month-old is in her playpen. When she starts to cry, her mother wants to pick her up and soothe her. But she's read a book by a renowned (male) expert that encourages her, "Teach her to find comfort and amusement in a teddy bear."

- A two-year-old stumbles, falls, and begins to cry. His mother wants to pick him up and comfort him. His father, like the (male) experts, is apt to say, "He's okay. Let him try again."

Throughout the world and throughout history, child-rearing has been the domain of women. Books of child-rearing advice written by men, on the other hand, first began to appear in England in the mid-1500s. In the early 1800s, child-rearing books written by men started to appear on the American market, among them *Letter to Ladies* by Dr. Thomas Ewell (1817) and *A Treatise on the Physical and Medical Treatment of Children* by Dr. William Potts Dewees (1838). *The Management of Infants, Physiological and Moral* by Dr. Andrew Combe came out in 1871, and a year later Dr. Combe published *The Mother's Guide for the Care of Her Children*. Gradually, the male experts began to gain popularity. By the turn of the century, the male doctor had established a solid foothold in the field of child-care advice, with Dr. Emmett L. Holt leading the way (his book, *The Care and Feeding of Children*, is still in print).

This shift in focus from women to men as the source of wisdom on early child care has resulted in conflict and confusion for mothers, fathers, and children. Should a child be encouraged to become independent and self-sufficient, and learn how to handle fears and loneliness on his own and as early as possible, as many men urge? Or should he be allowed free access to intimacy, closeness, and being held by his primary caretaker, as most mothers feel comfortable with? Should child rearing follow definite do's and don'ts and schedules? Or should a child proceed at his own pace, tackling ever more demanding tasks as he becomes ready to do so?

Conflicting ideas about raising children have led to a breakdown in communication between mothers and fathers, and mothers and doctors (especially male doctors), despite their shared goal of rearing emotionally stable children who are prepared for the complexities of the world. Some women have suffered from low self-esteem as mothers because their maternal feelings are not understood or appreciated—and, in fact, are often dismissed as wrong.

The insistence of many male experts on achieving independence as early as possible has undermined the bonding process between many a mother and child. This thwarting of the child's natural longing to be with his mother, especially during times of stress or loneliness, as well as of the mother's natural, often urgent, drive to give comfort, can create distress in both child and mother, because they are kept apart in time of want and need. It may also interfere with a child's natural development toward independence to enforce this ultimate goal too soon.

Meanwhile, the father's place in the child-rearing process has been all but ignored, leaving many fathers unsure as to whether they have a real role or what their importance is. Most child-rearing books give scant advice to fathers, usually little more than the equivalent of a pat on the back or "Be a good dad." A father is offered little or no insight into his wife's maternal emotions or her experience of mothering.

If the expert advice of men has created so much unhappiness, why do they continue to give it? The truth is that men—doctors and fathers—are just as concerned with the goal of child rearing as mothers are. They genuinely love their children and want to provide the best care and upbringing for them. The real question, I think, is, *Why* is there such a difference between men's and women's ideas about what constitutes the best care for children?—with one going by the calendar and the clock, the other by the readiness of the child; one seeking to encourage curiosity, taking on personal challenges, and an expansion of the child's world, and the other stressing nurturing, allowing the child to be held and cuddled when needed. And can these different approaches be made to complement, rather than conflict with, each other?

Today, when much information and research is becoming available about the fundamental differences between men and women, we owe it to our children to discuss the effects of these differences on our child-rearing practices and to reevaluate the advice of the male child-rearing experts. That is the goal of this book. The reader will begin to appreciate why men's and women's approaches differ and how each approach has a place in the child-rearing process, in balance with the growing child's needs. We will examine the source of the male experts' insistence that babies and young children be taught independence from early childhood on, often following a predetermined schedule, as well as of women's desire for intimacy with their children, in which enforced schedules and separation do not belong.

When we begin to understand and appreciate each other's emotions and values, we will be freed to see that, ideally, the male and female approaches to parenting can and should work together. It is important to encourage the acceptance of the mother's perspective, but it is not enough; we must also consider and appreciate the importance of the male approach.

When it comes to child rearing, most cultures do not operate on the basis of "mutual understanding"—they just simply "do," or follow tradition. But modern Western society no longer has a tradition in that sense. We have been analyzed and advised into total confusion, and have nothing to go on but forever-changing advice. Since we have no tradition to guide us, we need to approach these issues with an "understanding" instead. Mutual understanding will allow us to see, and to dedicate ourselves to, what is really important—meeting the needs of our children.

Chapter 1

The Mother Parenting versus Father Parenting Conflict

Men and women often differ in their approach to child rearing because of their different basic gender characteristics—not because one group is right and the other wrong, or one is wiser or more experienced than the other. When, for instance, a male doctor insists that a baby should be taught to play by herself by the age of eight months—to teach her independence—and her mother recoils at the thought of interrupting the intimacy she has with her child—feeling this is too early to begin enforced separation—both doctor and mother are voicing beliefs that feel right and valid to them. Each is expressing something that is a basic truth. The difference between their ideas of the truth is a reflection of what I refer to as a basic gender characteristic difference: the difference between men and women.

The most significant psychological difference between men and women is that men tend to be self-focused and seek independence, while women tend to be other-focused and seek intimacy and connectedness. This fundamental difference between the sexes manifests itself in many ways in our society. It is, I believe, the key to many of the conflicts that arise surrounding the raising of children.

In the hypothetical case above, the doctor would probably insist that his advice is based on the sound principle that teaching independence is crucial for the child. The mother, on the other hand, would probably believe that her opinion, based on strong feeling, makes more sense. The doctor would not understand why the mother wouldn't want to follow his advice; to him, it is an undeniable necessity that the child learn independence. The mother would be frustrated and confused because her doctor does not understand or appreciate her conviction that maintaining connectedness with her baby is what is right and that independence will follow naturally in due time. Because of her respect for the doctor, and perhaps the belief that he knows better than she—plus her desire to be a good mother in the eyes of others—she may begin to believe that her own feelings are wrong, and lose self-esteem and confidence as a mother. Often, women doubt that they know things even when they *do*, while at the same time they believe that the male experts know things even when they *don't*.

Susan enrolled her three-year-old daughter in a community nursery, but felt very uncomfortable about the child's obvious dislike of it and distress at the new experience. She expressed this concern to the nursery supervisor, who told her that research has shown that enforced separation for short periods of time leads to healthy independence in children. Only when she talked to other mothers who expressed the same concerns she had was Susan able to feel better about the validity of her own reaction. She decided to confront the situation and do what her heart told her: She took the child out, even though it was against "expert advice." Susan was fortunate that she was able to recognize her feelings and act upon them. All too often, such deep-rooted sources of conflict are never examined.

Some women end up simply ignoring their doctors or the child-rearing books when these experts stress the importance of enforced independence. Such mothers refuse to follow strict schedules in weaning or nighttime sleep habits. Michele Mason, a natural parenting instructor in California, told me, "I have found that when mothers become stronger in their conviction of motherhood, they just smile when their doctor tells them they should teach their child autonomy and independence. Then they go home and continue mothering their babies according to their own maternal feelings." This is a sad commentary on the level of communication between doctors and mothers, at a time when ideally they should be developing a level of trust and confidence. Another mother said that when her first child was born, she bought a copy of Dr. Benjamin Spock's *Baby and Child Care*. "But," she said, "he went so much against my feelings that I decided to go on my own intuition and not read another book on child rearing."

The conflict over different approaches to parenting is not limited to differences of opinion between mothers and doctors. Friction can develop between a wife and her husband, between mother and teacher, or anyone else involved with children and deciding what approaches are best for them. It can also develop between two women—whether teacher and mother, author and mother, or doctor and mother—when one of them strongly believes that independence is the primary goal in child rearing.

Both my personal observations and study of popular child-rearing books and syndicated columns have shown me that the different gender characteristics of men and women reveal themselves time and again and lead to confusion about parenting styles and attitudes toward child rearing, causing disagreements, anger, and tears.

When my first child, Yvonne, was six weeks old, I began to have problems putting her to bed. In the evenings, I attempted to set up the routine that was advocated in the child-rearing books: Nurse the baby, and when she has fallen asleep, put her in her bassinet. If she awakens during the night, go to her, nurse her, and put her down again in the bassinet. At no time allow her to sleep with you. This, I was warned, would lead to her becoming a very dependent and controlling child. The baby must, the books said, learn to sleep by herself and develop her independence. If necessary, let her cry for a few nights, and soon she will learn that at night, she is supposed to sleep, and to do so in her own bed.

I tried to be a good mother and follow the advice of the experts. But my baby had not read the books. For months, she continued to wake up when I put her down in her little bed. I had many fleeting thoughts of how simple it would be if I could just crawl into the crib with her, nurse her to sleep, and then quietly leave. But, of course, I didn't, because I was afraid that the crib would collapse under my weight. The thought of it made me giggle and feel frustrated at the same time. Meanwhile, I continued to nurse or rock the baby to sleep in my arms. Hardly daring to breathe, I'd tiptoe to her bed and ever so gently lower her onto a pre-warmed blanket, and then float out of the room. But sure enough, within minutes, I'd hear, "Mama!" At first it was nothing but a small whimper, but the translation was clear: "Please come!"

It was evident that Yvonne wanted to be held a great deal, and that nighttime was no exception. It would be so much easier, I thought, to have her sleep in our bed. But the books told me that I should not allow her to sleep with us under any circumstances. So I didn't. Some books did advise that I could, after she had cried awhile, go into her room. But if I did, I was to avoid making eye contact with her, and merely pat her briefly on the back, tell her every-thing was okay, and leave again. Why? Because it was important for her to learn self-reliance and independence.

Because I wanted to be a good mother, I tried this "crying it out" method. But I hated it. Inside me a voice cried, along with my baby's, "This is not right!" My arms ached to pick her up and bring her close to me. Then one day I decided, "Forget this. We'll find another way."

In a desperate attempt to find literature that would support my feelings, I began to check out books on child rearing from the library. I read every book and article I could lay my hands on. I was confronted by numerous methods and opinions, many of which caused me even more frustration and confusion. Many of the books told me that I should teach my children independence and self-reliance—at play time, at nighttime, at meal time, at babysitter time. They said that it was okay to let babies cry themselves to sleep; that it was good for a baby's self-es-teem for her to discover that she can handle loneliness on her own. They gave feeding schedules, sleep schedules, weaning schedules. Those books aroused anger in me, and I put them aside. It seemed to me generally meaningless—and heartless—to force a child to be independent and autonomous before she is ready to handle it.

I savored the few books that supported my feelings, the conviction that said, "If my child needs me, I should be there for her. Crying alone is not healthy." These books reinforced my belief that independence is gained through lots of loving, connectedness, and intimacy, not by forcing children to be on their own before they are ready. They gave me insight into the general developmental stages of children and encouraged me to listen to my child, not the clock. The advice of these authors felt right, but none of them were best-sellers on the American market. In the end, I followed my own feelings and went against the advice of the more popular books, but not without confusion, sometimes anger, and occasional feelings of guilt. Suppose I was wrong?

When one of my children was twelve years old, she had to have two teeth removed for an orthodontic program. She asked me to stay with her until she "went to sleep" before the operation. Arrangements were made with the dental office, and we understood that I would remain with her in the operating room. On the day of the operation, however, I was informed by the orthodontist that I had to leave the operating room. When I tried to explain to him that my daughter preferred for me to be with her, he told me that that was not possible. After some fruitless discussion, he said that these operations were entirely routine, and if my child was not able to handle this by herself, it was because I had failed to teach her independence and self-reliance.

We walked out of the office. I was hurt and angry and perplexed. From the birth of my first child on I had heard, "You've got to teach them independence and self-reliance." But something inside me did not believe this. I just could not see anything wrong with giving unconditional love and support to a child who needs it and asks for it. I couldn't see why it was supposed to be so much better and more admirable to be independent and self-reliant than to need and accept the support and comfort of others. I felt, in fact, that wanting to meet a child's needs was a positive quality in a parent. I did not force myself on her; I was simply available, and my self-assured child felt comfortable in asking me to stay with her. No shame there. But instead of feeling the doctor's acceptance and recognition, I sensed a definite judgment, of both my daughter and me, as incompetent and insecure. This bewildered me. Why were my feelings as a mother, my urge to be there for my child—especially during a time of great stress—so utterly misunderstood and rejected? And why all this unrelenting stress on independence?

Most mothers delight in seeing self-sufficiency in their children. A mother will beam as she talks about how comfortable her child is spending the night at a friend's house, going to kindergarten, or going to sleep by herself. At the same time, however, mothers see nothing wrong with maintaining an interdependent relationship—an intimacy, an openness to fulfilling a child's need for connectedness whenever it is expressed, whether she is six months old, three years old, twelve years old, or any other age. ·

SOURCES OF CONFLICT

The difference of opinion about independence and interdependence leads to many conflicts between husbands and wives. One father I know argued to his wife that their young child, Jason, should learn to accept being left in the church nursery, even if he protested. It would teach the little boy to rely on himself, he said, a feeling that would make the child feel good about himself. His wife hesitated. She felt uneasy about the arrangement. The father was following his own underlying beliefs, and he had the support of their male pediatrician, whose advice made perfect sense to him. But the mother couldn't understand how her husband could be so callous about their child's very real distress for the sake of teaching him something abstract. "This is not teaching independence," she contended. "This is showing Jason that we don't care." "But we're doing it because we *do* care," her husband countered.

The conflict between independence and interdependence surfaces as a cause of disagreement between husbands and wives in the issue of how often a mother should breast-feed a child, and when a child should be weaned. Sheri had a comfortable nursing relationship with her nine-month-old son, when her husband, with the support of their male pediatrician, told her that it was time to wean the baby. She was stunned and could not understand why she should have to force weaning at nine months when the nursing was going so well. Nursing seemed like such a natural thing to do, and both she and the baby enjoyed it. But her husband was adamant. Their pediatrician was adamant. Both men genuinely felt it was in the best interest of the child's sense of pride that he be weaned and no longer dependent on his mother for nourishment.

Sleeping arrangements are another area where husbands and wives frequently disagree. One mother, a television producer, told me that her husband at first agreed to allow their child, Erin, to sleep with them, but later began to question the idea. He wondered if it was wise, and finally decided that Erin should sleep in his own bed. As so often happens when two parents lock horns, their argument was conducted not with a feeling of, "We have different opinions," but rather, "I am right and you are wrong." Dad began to stress the importance of independence; mom stressed the importance of togetherness and comfort for the child. And the child himself, who should have been the center of their attention, was effectively shunted to the sidelines of this parental battle. As happens more often than not, the mother gave in to her husband for the sake of peace and the preservation of their relationship, even though she shuddered at seeing her child's needs go unmet. An African saying rather painfully sums it up: "When elephants fight, it is the grass that suffers."

Was this father being callous? No. Like most fathers, he cares very deeply about his son. He was merely advocating an approach that he felt would be best for the child. But he was doing so from a male perspective, not a maternal one.

The emphasis on schedules and timetables is another potentially frustrating feature of child-rearing advice given by men. Now, the orderliness of schedules sounds very good. If they worked, they would make of child rearing a wonderfully controlled exercise. And there are indeed some children whose personalities more or less allow for such a structured lifestyle. We have all heard of mothers whose children sleep through the night, who play for hours by themselves, who are content and ask for little. Those children are the envy of other mothers.

One mother from Australia wrote to me in desperation:

> The woman on the corner is four months pregnant and her other child is about 18 months. She says that her oldest one is so easy. Never complains or interrupts her sleep at night. Why does her baby follow the schedules while mine seems to want so much of our attention? It's exhausting. Don't get me wrong. She is a beaut [sic] child. But my husband keeps saying, "never again." Do many husbands say this or is it because I'm such a rotten mother and wife?

From the tone of the letter, I suspect it was written when this desperate mom was at the end of her rope. Perhaps she wrote it in the wee hours of the morning after a rough night, when one look out the window told her that, all down the street, everyone else was sleeping. But it is clear that she was tremendously bothered by the fact that her child did not follow the orderly timetables promoted by pediatricians and child-rearing books, and that both she and her husband were suffering because their expectation that their child should sleep through the night was unfulfilled.

I can speak firsthand of the difficulties with predetermined timetables. Right from the beginning, my own two children had very different temperaments. Yvonne, my first-born, needed a great deal of attention, constantly. Schedules meant nothing to her. My second child,

Michelle, was, as we boast in our culture, "so much easier." She fit easily into our family life. She was content to
play by herself as long as she was within eyesight of me.
While Yvonne became frustrated easily, Michelle rarely
cried. I probably would have had a fair amount of luck
with her if I had chosen to follow schedules. (I didn't. By
then, I was following the best piece of advice I'd ever
received: Turn your clocks to the wall and tune in to your
child instead.)

For many, if not most, mothers and children, schedules
just don't work without conflicts. Instinctively, many
mothers know that if a baby wants to be held, it is for a
reason. Schedules are, therefore, meaningless, and the rou-
tines are quickly forgotten because they don't fit the child's
needs. But abandoning the schedules often leads to other
conflicts for a mother—with her husband, her doctor, or
even within herself. She may be seriously torn between her
own emotions and the seemingly expert advice of others.

NOT RIGHT AND WRONG; MALE AND FEMALE

The question no one has ever told mothers and fathers to
ask is whether their difference of opinion lies not in right
versus wrong, but in male versus female. Especially in the
heat of conflict, when parents debate what is best for their
children, their positions can only be based on their own
individual interpretations of the situation, which are
formed in part by their gender characteristics. This makes
it difficult to focus on and get in touch with the actual
needs of an individual child in a particular situation. Yet
none of us can begin to figure out what is really best until
we first understand and accept the perspectives, emotions,
and reasons of others.

Unless we have done extensive study in the field of human
behavior, we tend to assume that other people reason in

essentially the same way we do, simply because our own way of thinking makes sense to us. When her husband or pediatrician dismisses a mother's concern that too much separation is making her child unhappy, she is likely to feel that her feelings have been rejected, and perhaps even that they are wrong. What seems like the rejection of her feelings rarely comes from an intent to reject, however. Generally, it is a product of a pair of assumptions on the man's part: first, that men and women have the same emotional responses; and second, that the well-educated scientist or trained physician, with years of clinical observation, will have more knowledge than an "untrained" mother. It is not that the so-called experts are against maternal feelings as such. But when mothers' emotions do not coincide with their own, they tend to believe that their own point of view makes more sense. Most men are not aware, nor does it ever occur to them, that women reason and make judgments differently than they do, and that women's feelings and beliefs—influenced by their gender and by their maternal condition—are as valid as their own—just different.

Neither science nor society has prepared them to see this. Until recently, the subject was rarely talked about, outside of the narrow field of human behavior studies. Indeed, the late 1960s and 1970s saw the proliferation of research that strongly supported the idea that there are no fundamental psychological differences between men and women. Recently, however, a more realistic discussion of the issue has been emerging and gaining increasing prominence. Best-selling books like *You Just Don't Understand: Women and Men in Conversation* by Deborah Tannen, Ph.D., and Carol Gilligan's *In a Different Voice* are bringing the awareness of gender differences to the popular level, and there is every indication that it will continue to be a topic of much discussion. Until this type of understanding has

permeated all levels of society, though, when a disagreement arises between a mother and her male pediatrician,
the doctor probably will not view the difference as being
between male and female, but between an educated,
trained physician and an inexperienced young mother
whose feelings and emotions cannot be taken too seriously. As one prominent male researcher in the 1970s said,
"It is well to have guidance from experts who are skillful
clinicians and scientists aware of the frontiers in the science and art of the care of the family of the normal and sick
newborn baby."[1] It seemed a foregone conclusion to him
that the experts in child care were scientists and clinicians,
not mothers.

It will probably take a long time before an understanding
of the real gender-based differences between men and
women has a direct impact on our daily lives. But all change
begins with awareness, and awareness leads to tolerance and
understanding. As Dr. Tannen writes, "A mutual acceptance
will at least prevent the pain of being told you are doing
something wrong when you are only doing things your
way."[2]

ARCHETYPES

At this point, an urgent clarification is needed. I wish to
make it very clear that I am discussing the *generic* man and
the *generic* woman, a pair of archetypes to which many
readers will relate easily (although some may not). One
must always be careful when talking in generalities, but I
feel that these archetypes provide some very revealing
insights into how we raise our children. For a time, during
the 1970s and early 1980s, "talk of inborn differences was
distinctly unfashionable, even taboo," as Christine Gor-
man wrote in the January 20, 1992 issue of *Time*. Differences between men and women were then held to be solely

a product of social conditioning. This was the era of unisex, when books like *Myths of Gender* by Anne Fausto-Sterling sought to prove that there is no difference between the sexes by pointing out, for instance, that women are just as intelligent as men. The focus was on attempting to erase the differences in order to increase respect for women, instead of seeking to understand the differences and promote mutual respect.

Since that time, however, many people have come to see that what is really needed is "a space in which to talk about the distinguishing characteristics of men and women without its being demeaning to either," as psychotherapist Robert May, Ph.D., wrote in 1980.[3] Perhaps the evolution in the recognition of gender differences followed a logical pattern. When women began, in the 1960s and 1970s, to object vociferously to being unappreciated and discriminated against in the male-dominated business world, it made sense to try to downplay gender differences, which were used to exclude women, in order to gain recognition for women's intelligence, capabilities, and contributions in the world outside the home. But we are now seeing a swinging of the pendulum in the direction of attempting to understand what the differences and similarities between men and women really are, and what they do (and do not) really mean. At last, an attempt is being made to see how we complement one another.

How much difference is there between the sexes? Niles Newton, Ph.D., once explained it visually. She held out both hands, palms down, fingers spread apart. She then slowly placed one hand partway over the other, so that most of the fingers overlapped but some did not. "My right hand is male and my left hand female," she said. "They are very much alike. They overlap a great deal. Yet they are different." There is tremendous strength in both hands working together.

Throughout this book references will be made to general characteristics of men and women, characteristics that have been recognized and validated through numerous anthropological, sociological, and psychological studies and observations. No one likes to be grouped or labeled, or swallowed up in a stereotype. But as Dr. Deborah Tannen once said in an interview, "If there are patterns [of gender differences], the danger of not identifying them is greater than the danger of identifying them. And it's women in particular who suffer if we don't describe the differences, because we have one standard in this country, and that standard is based on men's way."[4]

Some readers will argue that they know mothers who are very independent women, at home as well as in business outside the home. They know mothers who don't mind being separated from their children for a certain amount of time every day and night; women who much prefer the stimulation of the outside world, away from home and children. This is nothing new. Throughout history there have been mothers who preferred to spend at least some time away from their offspring; even ancient Babylonian records make reference to mothers who could afford to employ wet nurses, for example.[5] There are also mothers who support the idea that it is good for children to become self-sufficient at an early age. They may simply believe that self-sufficiency is a good thing, or they may need their children to be independent because their hectic schedules include a nine-to-five job in addition to taking care of a husband, home, and children.

On the other hand, there are men who are very close and loving with their children; men who will rush in to pick up a crying child; men who care tenderly for their babies, have their children sleep with them, and who allow their children total access to either themselves or their wives. One mother I know told me that, even though her husband had a very rough childhood and spent his first fifteen years in an orphanage, he was the most wonderful, caring man and father she had ever met in her life. In the book *Fathers*, a beautiful photograph of a father holding his child accompanies a thought by Lafcadio Hearn:

> No man can possibly know what life means, what the world means, what anything means, until he has a child and loves it. And then the whole universe changes and nothing will ever again seem exactly as it seemed before.[6]

So there are men who have received a great deal of emotional fulfillment in seeing the intimate bond between mother and child, just as there are men who take delight in watching their children grow up, without pressuring or hurrying them. Obviously, all men are not alike, and neither are all women. When I refer to general or generic or gender-specific characteristics, I recognize that there are innumerable differences within, as well as between, the two groups. But while men and women have a great deal in common, there are nevertheless basic gender characteristic differences. Each of us is an individual, but most of us display these definite gender characteristics to a greater or lesser extent.

OTHER PARENTING INFLUENCES

Gender, of course, is not the only thing that determines a parent's approach to child rearing. Many other influences come into play. Individual personality traits lead some people, men and women alike, to be people-oriented, tending to seek interaction. Others have a greater need for solitude. Even though these people may love children, especially their own, they may have less need or desire to connect intimately with them for long periods of time.

Some people are task-oriented and thrive on achieving goals; they may naturally encourage their children to do likewise. Other people are feeling-oriented and base their feelings of accomplishment on having rewarding relationships. Some are competitive and status-oriented; others are interested in working cooperatively for the benefit of all. Some people are detail-oriented, while others prefer to focus on the big picture and leave the details to someone else. Some are leaders, initiators, and entrepreneurs; others are more comfortable as followers, carrying out the ideas of others. All of our individual traits and values will affect the way we interact with our children.

External factors, such as family, job, or financial stress, can greatly influence one's approach to raising children. So can peer pressure and societal pressure. Many men, for example, feel pressure to appear tough and dominant because that is what they have been told a man is supposed to be. Women can feel pressure to be the "supermom" who is praised for doing everything and "having it all." Our own childhoods, the cultures and families we were raised in, and our own parents' child-rearing styles also greatly influence our approach to our children. Some people, consciously or unconsciously, emulate their parents. Others remember less-than-happy childhood experiences and make every effort to avoid repeating with their own children what they themselves endured. The relationship between a husband and wife, and their relationship to their children as a family, as well as each of their relationships with each individual child, will all affect the way they raise their children. If a child is raised by a single parent, that too influences the approach.

But in spite of all the differences—social standards and customs, family environment, personalities, one's own childhood experiences—*generally, generically* men and women have recognizable, and different, tendencies. And we are living in an era when, although most children are cared for by women, most of those considered to be child-care experts are men. When men tell women how to rear young children, they do it from an essentially male perspective that for the most part ignores women's feelings and values, particularly the strong impulse toward maintaining intimacy and a sense of connectedness. The result is tension, confusion, and stress for all concerned, but most of all for women—who often hear the implied message that their emotions and beliefs are wrong, and that they should deny them—and for children, who need a great deal of nurturing that they simply will not receive if both parents behave the way the male experts tell them to.

Some readers may be inclined to argue that by raising the subject of gender differences, I am pitting men against women, or portraying women as victims—or perhaps even that it is nonsense to talk about the subject at all. But there are basic differences, and they are significant. Our real concern should be to understand them, and to see how they operate in the way we raise our children. Understanding will lead to greater cooperation, an appreciation of each other's point of view, and perhaps even awe at the marvelous diversity of individuals and the dance of life that happens between them. It will liberate both mothers and fathers by endowing them with a greater feeling of self-worth, and will help them to realize that each parent has a vital and unique part to play in a child's life.

Throughout history, men and women—and especially men—have written down their thoughts about child rearing. These thoughts in many instances reflect the times in which the authors lived. They also seem to reflect a definite gender difference. In this boxed inset, as well as in others that can be found throughout the book, you will find some revealing perspectives on child rearing.

"The rod and reproof give wisdom,
but a child left to himself
brings shame to his mother."

The Book of Proverbs

"As he spared his rod,
he hated his child."

Aelfric (c. 1000)
Anglo-Saxon monk and writer

"Mothers say 'no' to no request. They let
[their children] have their way; they take their side
when they complain about the hurts of their
playmates or the blows of their teachers, just as if . . .
they themselves were injured. Finally, they allow them
complete license for whatever they want. . . .
What could be more monstrous than this easy and
permissive education, which mothers in particular
are wont to follow?"

Maffeo Vegio
Fifteenth-century Florentine poet

Chapter 2

Understanding Basic Gender Differences

In ancient Greek mythology, the goddess mother Demeter roams the earth in agony trying to find her daughter, Persephone, and only finds happiness again when the two are reunited. In another myth, the young Phaethon tries to convince his father Phoebus, the sun god, to allow him to drive the chariot of the sun. Phoebus tells the youth that he is not ready to take the reins, but his son perseveres and wins out. He takes off, but in his wild, daring challenge discovers that he cannot control the horses, and ultimately plunges to his death.

"Myths," writes psychotherapist Dr. Robert May, "are fantasies shared by a whole culture. [They are tales] that embody important concerns . . . of what matters in human life. Such stories are shaped over centuries and only survive if they continue to have an important common appeal."[1] The truths in these ancient myths can still speak to us today. The myth of Demeter plays on a female gender characteristic, the need for connectedness and intimacy, especially between mother and child. The young Phaethon portrays the male gender characteristic of independence and challenge-seeking.

Western psychologists started writing about the differences between the sexes the moment they started doing research. But the vast majority of this research has been conducted and documented based on a male point of view. Men have generally been taken as the norm and women considered a deviation from that norm. No doubt this is, in part, because until quite recently men were the primary researchers, philosophers, and authors, and many of them looked upon women as intellectually and emotionally inferior to men. They did realize that without a woman's work and contributions in the home, home would hardly be worth returning to. Women had the heavy resonsibilities of cooking, bearing and caring for children, making clothes, tending vegetable and herb gardens, and teaching children, and, when their husbands were away at war or on business, they assumed full management of the land and household.[2] So mental health and well-being for women came to be synonomous with how well they performed in this role, rather than being based on women's own values and emotions. In 1929, Virginia Woolf observed that even though the values of men and women differ frequently, it is the masculine values that prevail.[3] And women's principal occupation, homemaking, did not produce the research, money, power, or recognition that would have been required to change this perception.

Men, on the other hand, lived primarily outside the home and excelled in whatever it took to "bring home the bacon." Since it was outside the home that formal academic and scientific work took place, this reinforced the tendency of research to be male-oriented. Although they were needed on the home front, women were considered less intelligent and less capable of sophisticated moral development than men, and were simply not included in most of the studies.

Fortunately, in the past several decades a number of researchers have started taking a closer and more serious look at the differences between men and women, including their communication styles, their approaches to a variety of life's situations, and their inherent strengths. Much of the impetus for this research came from the influence of the women's movement. What researchers are "discovering"is that women are no less intelligent than men, nor are they inferior in any other mental or psychological areas, but they *are* distinctly different from men. Such insights are frequently fascinating to women—not because they are new, but because they elicit a response of, "You're describing what I've always felt!"

In a sense, then, this research is merely validating something that many people have always known but never talked about. Especially from women, the open discussion of the subject often elicits an "Aha!" response—a sigh of relief, a burst of knowing laughter, or a cry of "Yes!" This is a heartfelt response to the fact that, finally, their feelings are being recognized and, more important, are being accepted as normal and valid.

For example:

> Bob and Jackie are going to a party. They were given directions, but somehow they get lost along the way on lonely streets. Then Jackie sees another person walking down the street. Relieved, she says to Bob, "Oh, there's someone. Let's ask for directions.""No," he replies. "We'll find it on our own."

Many people can't help but smile when they hear this story. Why? Because they can relate to it. During my college years, a similar experience caused my date and me to be half an hour late to a dinner party. According to Dr.

Deborah Tannen, professor of linguistics at Georgetown University and best-selling author, this common example points to a very real, very basic difference between men and women.

Women seem to naturally feel a sense of connectedness to others. They see nothing wrong with forming a bond, even momentarily, with another person. Women tend to thrive on connectedness yet retain their sense of independence in the process. As Cris Evatt, author of *He and She*, writes, "Women see themselves primarily in relation to people around them and their sense of self comes from this relatedness."[4] In keeping with this, Jackie sees asking a stranger for directions as making contact with a fellow person, not as an admission that she is dependent or weak.

Men, on the other hand, usually thrive on independence. It is their way of realizing and feeling strength and self-respect. "[A man's] sense of self," Evatt continues, "comes from pitting himself against others in a process of individuation."[5] Bob does not want to become dependent on another person, even momentarily, to achieve his goal, and so does not want to ask for directions.

INDEPENDENCE AND HIERARCHY VERSUS INTERDEPENDENCE AND INTIMACY

Independence is very important to most men. One of their greatest fears is that they may become dependent on others, and not able to "stand on their own two feet." For women, the need to be utterly self-sufficient is far less strong. It is difficult to separate oneself from cultural prejudice in examining these concepts, and, as I have pointed out, the values of our culture have so far been determined mostly by men's values. But if we take a step back from the assumption that independence must be a virtue, can we objectively determine that there is, in fact, something inherently good about independence and undesirable about interdependence?

Any examination of human behavior starts from the fact that people, whoever they are and in whatever situation, adopt strategies designed to get them what they need or want. In order to understand why it is that independence is such a vital concern for men, but not for women, we must ask what it is that being independent achieves in men's lives that it apparently does not achieve in women's.

One of the reasons men give most frequently for valuing independence is that it creates self-esteem. But healthy self-esteem is important for both sexes. After all, a woman wouldn't be likely to say, "I don't need to be independent because *I don't need* self-esteem. She would, however, be likely to say, "I don't need to be independent *in order to have* self-esteem." The average man would not agree with either statement. He would be more likely to say, "I *do* need to be independent in order to have self-esteem." And both would be right.

What is going on here? The answer lies in the different ways men and women relate to other people and find their places in society. Men's concepts of social units and interactions tend to be precisely hierarchical. Robert Bly, the celebrated poet who is considered a leader of the modern American men's movement, said in an interview: "Men love hierarchy. Long for hierarchy. Feel good in hierarchy. Hierarchy is very beautiful."[6] Men are almost always acutely aware of status—their own and everyone else's—and interactions with other people are essentially a process of negotiating to enhance, or at least defend, their status. This isn't necessarily hostile. Consider a casual, friendly conversation between two men. If one starts by saying, for instance, that he just spent half an hour stuck in slow-moving traffic, more likely than not his companion will respond by saying something like, "That's nothing. Last week I got caught in a traffic jam so bad I couldn't move at all for an hour." This is a sort of friendly verbal competition, a jockeying for position. In this case, status is achieved by having endured a more trying road trip than the other guy.

Women, on the other hand, have a more egalitarian, interdependent social style. When it comes to interacting with others, they tend to value relating to people and measure success by the depth and strength of their connections. Two women might have a similar conversation to that of the two men above, but with a very important difference: After the first one told about the half-hour delay, her companion would probably say something like, "What a pain. Doesn't it drive you nuts when that happens?" This is a process of making or strengthening a connection. Whereas the hidden message of the men's talk might be expressed as, "I've endured worse traffic than you have," the hidden message of the women's conversation would be, "That's happened to me, too. I know how you feel."

In the male, hierarchical world, if a man lacks or loses independence, it places him in an inferior position. If you depend on someone else, your status is lowered and the other person's is enhanced. So if you ask for directions, for instance, you lower yourself in the hierarchical order. Women, however, are less concerned about independence but are more afraid of losing or breaking their connections with other people. This is where their greatest satisfaction—their self-esteem—comes from. Asking for help does not usually cause a woman to lose self-esteem, because her self-esteem was never based on avoiding it to begin with. In fact, for women, expressing needs or asking for help can actually be a positive thing because in many circumstances it can lead to a strengthening of those all-important ties to other people.

Which view is "correct"? They both are. But it is important to realize that men's reasoning is right *for men* and women's reasoning is right *for women*. If our culture could generally accept this, things would be very different. As it is, men often see women's desire or need to be with others as dependent (and therefore, in their view, inferior), not as reasonable and healthy. "It is a testimony to the male bias of our society that such qualities are often referred to with the demeaning names of 'dependence' or 'conformity,'" writes Dr. Robert May in *Sex and Fantasy.*[7]

This begins to explain why the orthodontist insisted that I had failed to teach my daughter independence. He saw my child's need for me, and my willingness to provide her comfort during a time of stress, as dependent behavior. In fact, I was simply following the characteristic female behavior of striving for connectedness.

Likewise, it begins to shed light on the frustration experienced by so many mothers when their desire for nurturing, bonding, and closeness with their children, from birth on, is misunderstood by men. It also explains why predetermined schedules and timetables for weaning, eating, playing, sleeping, and enforced separation have no meaning for so many mothers. When women do not want to be separated from their infants or children, it does not necessarily mean they are overly protective or standing in the way of their children's growing independence. They are just being mothers, and to them it feels right. It feels right to children, too, because, as we shall see, children need an abundance of both love *and* connectedness.

So while women tend to see people as mutually dependent and see nothing wrong with picking up a crying baby or comforting a child who has difficulty falling asleep, men tend to view people as independent and see nothing wrong with encouraging a crying baby or fretful child to discover his own self-reliance and independence. One mother I know said her husband had no problem teaching children early independence when it came to sleeping. His justification: "It will make your life easier. You can't be around all the time, and it will give them a tremendous sense of accomplishment." She wanted to believe him and tried to follow his advice. After all, it certainly would have been nice if their children could be more self-sufficient. But to achieve this autonomy by means of forced separation and tears just did not make sense to her. In fact, she was amazed that her husband could listen to a child's crying and do nothing, while she felt utterly miserable and agitated at hearing the distraught child.

Another mom related an incident that occurred at their home, when their six-year-old had fallen on the ice on his way out the door to catch the school bus. He came back inside, crying, wanting to stay home until he felt better. To mom, that posed no problem. But her husband, after observing that nothing was broken or seriously injured, insisted that his son go on his way: "He should learn to be a big boy, and big boys are tough." Mother wanted to connect and soothe and nurture. Father wanted to encourage his child to display masculine independence. And both parents were "right," based on their own specific gender characteristics.

SEPARATENESS AND COMPETITION VERSUS TOGETHERNESS AND COOPERATION

Characteristic gender differences can be noted soon after birth. For example, by the second or third day after birth, infant girls generally maintain eye contact with adults for twice as long as baby boys do. By the age of four months, most girls will respond to photographs of familiar faces, while boys generally don't.

By the end of the first year, more overtly recognizable

differences emerge. Girls tend to remain in closer proximity to their mothers, while boys are already showing signs of their gender-specific need for independence and exploration. They wander farther away and show more vigorous, muscular activity in play.[8] According to research cited by Carol Gilligan in *In a Different Voice*, gender identity has been firmly and irreversibly established, for both sexes, by the time a child is around three.[9] From that time on, most boys begin a definite breaking away from the close association with and dependence on their mothers to develop their identity and independence within a hierarchical arena. They vie for positions of importance or leadership, a process that is necessary for their male gender development. Girls, on the other hand, continue to develop their inherent and gender-specific tendency for close, interdependent relationships.[10] Cris Evatt found that preschool girls spend an average of three times as long saying goodbye to their mothers as boys do. They are also more likely to sit quietly and play with or cuddle a doll, while boys usually show a greater interest in aggressive motions such as pushing a toy car or train around. And when a newcomer comes to school, girls will generally greet their new classmate and form some sort of connection, while boys usually maintain an attitude of indifference.[11]

The games that children play tend to show gender-specific characteristics. When boys are given a large box to play with, they may use it as a fortress to protect themselves from the "enemy," while girls would make a home out of it. This is what psychoanalyst Erik Erikson described as "caution outdoor" (male), and "goodness indoor" (female) themes. Boys' games are often competitive, with rules and regulations to adhere to. Boys are more likely to play outside in large groups, with one being the leader (Superman or king of the mountain) and with elaborate rules that ultimately result in clear winners and losers. To challenge others for position within their groups, boys often boast of their skill and talk at great length about who is best at what.[12] Given a chance, most boys, like most men, will try to engage others in a challenge, whether physical or verbal, to prove themselves better than others. In order to be a leader, or challenge a leader, one has to be independent and willing to move up (or risk moving down) in a hierarchical situation. Interdependence or intimacy would not allow them to negotiate for status within their social milieu.

While boys are challenging each other and the outside world, girls tend to play in small, intimate groups with a few best friends. Their preferred activities, such as playing house, jumping rope, playing hopscotch, or just sitting and talking for hours on end, do not allow for clear winners or losers.[13] One study noted that three- and four-year-old girls are much more likely than boys to choose a telephone as a toy and hold long conversations either with each other or by themselves.[14] Instead of competing for leadership roles and center stage, girls tend to emphasize cooperative play; instead of devising rules and regulations, girls prefer negotiation, making sure they are liked by their peers in the process.

Obviously, some girls are more aggressive and some boys more nurturing than others. Some families and cultures are more and some less supportive or tolerant of gender-specific traits. "But," writes Rita Kramer in *In Defense of the Family*, "unless one is guided by a political agenda requiring a society in which as few distinctions as possible remain between individuals or groups, it is hard to deny that sex-linked biological predispositions exist. In other words, sexual stereotypes have some biological basis in reality."[15] Or, as Anne Moir and David Jessel more boldly state in *Brain Sex*, to maintain "that [women and men] are the same in aptitude, skill and behavior is to build a society based on a biological and scientific lie."[16]

As to whether behavioral differences between girls and boys are brought about by the outside influences of mothers or society, Dr. Robert May cites numerous studies that indicate "[what] mothers could have told us years ago," namely that there are many ways in which the child controls or influences the mother's behavior toward her child, rather than the other way around.[17] Mothers respond to their children's needs, personalities, and gender characteristics. A mother will naturally hug and hold a baby more if the child requests it. On the other hand, her response cannot be as intimate if her child will not allow it.

For girls to develop a feminine identity, they do not have to break away from their mothers in the way that boys do. They continue their connectedness and attachment throughout their development and, to a large extent, throughout their lives.[18] A girl usually can, and does, rely on her friends; her cooperative relationships with them serve to reinforce interdependent behavior. From childhood on, many girls form close relationships with others, oriented around personal needs and feelings. They therefore usually develop an ability to experience the needs and feelings of others, as well as their own. As adults, they will call on this quality in their relationships with their own children.

This is the basic gender characterististic that I followed (unknowingly at the time) when I asked a school principal to allow my daughter to go through school with a few close friends in her constantly changing class. I felt it was important to develop intimacy and connectedness and wanted my child to experience this. When she was in the third grade, her classes were moved to a much larger school building. There were now four third-grade classes instead of one. After the first day of school, she told me that not one of her friends was in any of her classes, and asked me if there were some way for her to be together with her friends.

I went to see the principal. Dr. Peterson was a very nice

man, but he didn't understand why I felt so strongly about my daughter needing to be with friends. "She will make new friends," he encouraged. "Isn't it better for children to learn to make new friends? Isn't it much better for her to have many friends instead of a few close ones? Isn't it better for her to learn to be independent and self-reliant, instead of depending on a small clique of girlfriends?" It made sense on the surface. Yet I thought about my own childhood. I grew up in a small village and went to a small school, with a small, intimate group of girlfriends. That experience has not made me asocial or made it difficult for me to meet new friends. I told Dr. Peterson I thought it would be much better for Yvonne to go through school with a few truly close girlfriends than to have to make new friends every year and never have a chance to establish solid, long-term relationships. He did not agree with my argument, but he did agree to move her to another classroom with some of her previous schoolmates.

I now see that Dr. Peterson was not wrong when he urged that my daughter learn to be independent and make many friends instead of a few. He was giving me advice that reflected the way he would approach child rearing, based on the male gender characteristic that stresses the importance of independence. Had I understood that at the time, I might have been less tempted to shake my head and say, "How can he be so lacking in understanding of something that is so obvious and good?" Only recently have I come to understand what our difference really was, and with understanding comes a greater ability to accept the feelings of others.

INFORMATION VERSUS INTERACTION

The common conception that men "talk shop" is based on an underlying truth. For most males, the function of conversation is primarily to give or receive information, or to negotiate for status in a hierarchical order. Many men thrive on the type of communication in which they can transmit knowledge or demonstrate their expertise. This type of talk feels good to them because it accomplishes both of their conversational goals at once; it not only conveys information, but also enhances their status by establishing them as authoritative.

When conversation isn't clearly about information, many men can become frustrated. For instance, when a father is confronted with a sulking child, he may ask, "What's the matter?" If the child doesn't answer, he may feel frustrated, and then angry, reasoning that if the child cannot give him information about why he is unhappy, there must be nothing to sulk about.

Men often find it easier to relate to their offspring once they can begin to communicate verbally. The interaction with their children becomes more meaningful to them once they no longer have to rely on nonverbal clues to find out what's going on. "Dick left early child rearing to me," said Karen. "When our baby couldn't talk yet, he didn't know what to do with her." Once their child reached the age of three or four, her husband became actively involved in child care. Many fathers enjoy the type of communication with their children in which they can impart knowledge, such as showing how to fix, build, or operate something. This is the kind of talk (giving useful information) that seems meaningful to men, and acting as a teacher places them in a role that feels clearly defined, comfortable, important, and enjoyable.

For women, talk is for establishing connections, intimacy, and rapport. Women use talk to support one another. When they give information, it is often because it makes them feel good to be able to help others, not because it establishes them in a position of status in a hierarchy. The common saying that women chit-chat and talk about their feelings is also based on an underlying truth. To many men, it seems that women talk endlessly about inconsequential things—children's antics, what to wear to a party, little problems or joys, a new decoration for the home, relationships at work. But to women, the topic is not nearly as important as the interaction, the connection that conversation provides.

Most mothers can carry on animated "conversations" with their babies and young children, using mere sounds rather than logically constructed sentences. What is happening is not an exchange of information, but the weaving of an invisible connection carried on the babble of nonsensical words. I used to laugh with my good friend, Hazel, who went on forever with her nonsense words with both of her infant daughters. I used to tell her, "Those kids of yours are going to grow up talking like that." Little did I realize at the time that Hazel was simply following an essentially female and maternal way of deepening her bond with her daughters.

As a result of underlying gender characteristics, a man and a woman can be speaking the same language, but having, in effect, two different conversations. Dr. Deborah Tannen sums it up this way: "To him, talk is for information. [But] to her, talk is for interaction."[19]

SOLUTIONS VERSUS SUPPORT

Many people look at child rearing primarily as a matter of finding the correct solutions to a succession of problems. This, too, is a characteristically male approach. Men usually are more pragmatic in orientation than women are; by and large, it is their nature to try to identify problems and give solutions. This advice-giving approach allows a man to demonstrate his expertise and place himself in a dominant position with respect to the person receiving the advice.

Not surprisingly, then, as far as most men are concerned, when women talk to them about problems, it means that they are asking the men to solve them. Further, the male idea of a solution usually involves taking some kind of action, so, when confronted with other people's problems, they tend to prescribe actions. What women are often seeking, though, is not so much solutions to their problems as support, empathy, and reassurance. They want to hear, "I know how you feel" (or perhaps, from a male doctor, "I don't know how you feel, but I will try to understand"). They need to feel that they have the support and understanding of those around them. Sometimes they need this support far more than a solution itself. After all, if a suggested solution doesn't work, a woman can be left with frustration, feeling alone and like a failure. And, in fact, there *aren't* always solutions to the problems we face. But if a woman is given support and feels that other people share her problem or situation, she has that support to fall back on. Then, even if the solution doesn't work, she can remain connected with others through their empathy. The support of others helps a woman to "hang in there," to persevere despite whatever problems she faces. This is why women often find mothering support groups like La Leche League International, or any of the local support groups, more helpful than books on child rearing or their doctors' advice. A mother who has supportive friends who are also parents, with whom she can feel connected, often copes much better than one who relies strictly on problem-solving advice.

When a woman tells her doctor or her husband about a problem, she may simply want affirmation and understanding. One husband I know came home from a hectic day at the office to find his wife near tears. He asked her what the matter was. She told him that the children had gotten into a fight and then one of them had thrown up all over the couch, the dishwasher had broken down, she had received a nasty call about an unpaid bill, part of dinner had been burned in the preparation, and she was feeling pressured to "volunteer" for a church job. And just before her husband came home, their toddler had walked out of the yard and wandered down the block, where he was seen by a neighbor before she rescued him. For a few minutes, her husband stood in the kitchen, listening to her. Then, exasperated, he asked, "Well, what do you want me to do about it? Do you want me to quit my job and help you out?" His wife looked at him, perplexed. "No," she answered, "of course not. I just want you to listen to me and hear me and allow me to share my feelings with you." She didn't want a solution. She wanted support.

This difference between wanting solutions and wanting support may be what's behind the complaint of some male pediatricians that mothers fail to follow their advice. A doctor will often come up with a solution to a child-rearing problem, but his patient may just want to talk about the problem and nothing more. Women seek the support of others because giving and receiving empathy is a basic female gender characteristic.

BEING RESPECTED VERSUS BEING LIKED

Girls and women tend to be very concerned about being liked by their peers and keeping relationships harmonious. According to Dr. Deborah Tannen, being disliked is often a devastating experience for them, because of their need for affiliation.[20] Most men, on the other hand, are far more concerned about being respected. Wanting respect is a natural outcome of self-focus, according to Cris Evatt.[21] When a man feels respected, it validates his position in his hierarchical world and makes him feel good.

This may explain why it is that women often try to

follow prescribed child-rearing practices even if they go against their emotions and cause them a great deal of anguish. More than one mother has told me that she enforced separate sleeping, let her child cry himself to sleep, and forced him to handle stressful situations on his own, because "the book (or the doctor, or my husband) told me I should teach him independence." I spoke to a mother in California after an earthquake had occurred, damaging her home. The experience had greatly upset her five-year-old, who refused to sleep or play alone afterwards. A special earthquake pamphlet designed for caretakers of children—parents, teachers, child-care workers—advised that even though a child may have experienced emotional stress, it would be a mistake to allow him the comfort of his parents' bed. "Offer your support, but not your bed," was the message. This mother's need to feel accepted as a good mother was as strong as the pain her child's tears brought her. She was torn by the conflict, and by the message that she would "ruin that child" if she hovered over him too much. The acceptance of others is very important to women. They want to be considered good mothers, and if this means giving in to the demands of society, or husbands, or doctors, rather than following their hearts, many mothers will comply, even though something deep inside them tells them it just isn't right.

One male doctor told me he that he believes some parents, especially mothers, are sensitive to criticism if their children sleep with them, or nurse past a certain age, because they subconsciously feel guilty about doing something that is not healthy for the child. This is why they often won't speak about it openly, he said. I believe, however, that when women won't talk about such things, they may indeed be afraid of being criticized, but not because they feel guilty; rather, they know they may not be following cultural norms, and they fear being ostracized by society, by their families, by their neighbors, or by their doctors. So to avoid a possible break in connectedness and belonging, they choose not to talk about the subject. Above all, they want to be liked, to receive approval for their efforts, to be admired and praised as good mothers.

When fathers, on the other hand, avoid talking about family sleeping or extended breast-feeding, it is more likely to be because they feel they would risk losing the respect of their peers, their friends, or their doctors. As a matter of fact, a man may carry this avoidance one step further, insisting that the doctor's or society's advice be followed in the home so that he does not risk losing respect, even in his own mind.

FREEDOM VERSUS FREEDOM

"The sooner your baby becomes independent, the sooner you will have your freedom," say some men to mothers. But what is meant by freedom? For most men, freedom from the responsibility of children means freedom from obligations, not being tied down, having more time for oneself. Men usually want some intimacy, but only up to a point; too much of it and they may feel smothered. For men, therefore, training a child to sleep through the night, to wean early from the breast, to play by himself, to be toilet-trained, or to be able to sleep overnight at a friend's house—in other words, to be more independent—is a wonderful thing because it "frees you up."

For a woman, however, freedom from the responsibility of children usually means not having to worry about them being happy, content, and safe. But if her child needs her, her innate feeling of connectedness and desire to nurture arises. My four-year-old once asked me if I stayed up all night. When I responded, "Why?" she said, "Because all I have to do is say, 'Mama,' and you're right there." I answered, "That's the way mamas are."

To some men, gaining "freedom" is so important that they will insist their still-nursing wives to go away for "just a weekend." More than one mother has told me that she went along with her husband's plan, only to find that instead of enjoying a weekend away from her baby, she suffered from breasts that burned with milk tension, in addition to constant thoughts and worry about her child. Her husband, meanwhile, could not comprehend her intense bond with her child, or the break in connectedness that she experienced. Her worry about the child's safety and happiness made no sense to him, since the baby was being cared for by a competent babysitter. For him, freedom meant freedom from a young baby's intense and constant need for attention. To her, though, freedom would have meant freedom from worry. Going away caused a break in her bond with her child, which resulted in worry and emotional as well as physical tension—making her feel anything but free. She experienced the additional stress, in keeping with her characteristically female desire to be liked, of trying to please her husband and fulfill his unrealistic expectation that the outing would be glorious. Needless to say, the much-anticipated romantic weekend dissolved in total disaster.

THE CONSEQUENCES OF DIFFERENCE

Generally speaking, then, men approach life's situations from a perspective that focuses on the self, emphasizing independence, dominance, communication for information, and hierarchical relationships. Women's lives are generally shaped by a focus on relationships with others, so they place a greater value on interdependence, nurturing, communication for interaction, and cooperative relationships.

If we look at a woman in the role of a mother, we can see how well this preference suits her. During pregnancy, she is intimately connected with her unborn child. Just as oceanic research is now finding that the seas are far from silent, much data is beginning to show how aware the unborn child is of sounds, movement, and the motions and surroundings of the mother. There is every indication that the baby begins to have an awareness of his connectedness with his mother in utero, and at quite an early stage.[22]

After giving birth, a woman will usually experience an overwhelming desire for closeness with her child. Perhaps stronger than any other feeling is the emotional, physical, and spiritual bond she has with her child. There are times when women want and need some independence. But the innate female drive for intimacy, connectedness, and interdependence is apparent. Of course, men too need intimate relationships. In their book *What Men Are Like*, John Stanford and George Lough stress that a man can most successfully be independent when he knows that a secure network of relationships awaits him at home.[23] But while all people need both intimacy and independence, women tend to focus on the first and men on the second.

Men thrive on jockeying for position. A friend of mine, Jim, told me that after he comes home from a vigorous basketball game his wife always asks him, "Did you have fun?" Laughingly, he said, "That just bugs me. I want her to ask me, 'Did you win?' Playing is only fun if you have a chance to win." Because most males live in a hierarchical world, where the achievement of status and fighting to avoid being the underdog are of foremost importance, they must, by necessity, be independent and self-focused. This keeps them in touch with where they stand in relation to others.

This characteristic male competitiveness is present in many of the child-rearing books written by men, although it is not usually presented as such. But babies are measured and gauged on comparative scales, in such areas as weight gain, their ability to handle aloneness, their ability to eat by themselves, sleep by themselves, walk by themselves, and on and on. The need to compare and compete has been so impressed on our culture that a typical birth announcement, in addition to telling us the baby's name and sex, usually announces the child's weight and length. Perhaps at one time size was an indication of the health of the infant, and so conveyed the information that the little newcomer was strong and healthy. But surely today, when most babies born in the Western world are, indeed, healthy at birth, these details are really superfluous, except that we are so focused on the (characteristically male) competitive need for bigger and better.

Men tend to engage in competition for the sake of evaluating themselves against others. For many women, however, cooperation is more important; they care less about winning than men do.[24] This does not mean that women cannot enjoy competition. It is exhilirating and can bring out the best in us. But for women, the excitement often lies more in feeling good about a job well done. Years ago I participated in a long-distance cross-country ski race. As I was nearing the end, after four grueling hours of skiing, I became aware of another skier, a man, who was attempting to pass me and beat me to the finish line. Spurred on by the challenge, I was flooded with a surge of energy and thought to myself, "I'll give him a run for his money!" By this time, we were side by side, poling as hard as we could, narrowing the gap between us and the colorful flags at the end. The crowd began to cheer and I began to giggle. I was having fun. The harder I pushed, the more I giggled—until, just yards from the finish, I was laughing so hard that I fell and slid across the scraggly red line in the snow. My competitor won. But it felt good to have been forced to do the very best I could for the sake of the competition, and I enjoyed it. For women, competition can even become a form of cooperation, because it adds a flavor of fun that they can enjoy *together with* their competitors. This would seem contradictory to most men, who view competition as a means of achieving status in a hierarchical world by *distinguishing themselves from* their competitors.

The fundamental differences in the ways that men and women relate to others and to the world can be found in every culture that has been studied. In most societies, there is a gender-based division of labor, wherein women are the primary caretakers of children and men engage in activities requiring greater physical strength. If violence is part of a culture, it is a male specialty. In the overwhelming majority of cultures, men wield more authority than women, and women excel in nurturing, caretaking, and showing responsibility. Men engage in more aggressive and dominant behavior, and women are more concerned with conforming to social norms.

Cross-cultural research demonstrates that fundamental gender characteristics are found in people all over the world. These natural differences only turn into difficulties when we are instructed to ignore our own characteristics and adopt those of others. It is difficult, says Carol Gilligan in *In a Different Voice*, to use the word "different" without also implying better or worse, right or wrong. And in our society, which has had a strong tendency to regard male behavior as the norm, it has been difficult for women to have their feelings understood or accepted. The male way of thinking has been valued, while the female way has been regarded as deficient. So when women do not conform to male standards or expectations—whether in banking or baking, in law or in child rearing—the conclusion has generally been that their knowledge or reasoning is faulty.[25] Women, in this case mothers, are all too familiar with the inner conflict this creates, and may ask the desperate question, "Am I doing it all wrong?" when confronted with advice that contradicts their feelings or opinions.

It is an immense relief when you come to understand that there are few wrongs or rights here, but merely many manifestations of personalities and interpretations—and gender characteristics. When we understand some of the basic differences between men and women, we can look at two different child-rearing books and begin to understand why the author of one emphasizes adherence to schedules and encouraging a child to become autonomous, while the other gives insight into the general growth patterns of children, their needs, their fears, and wants, and approves of holding and unconditionally loving a child. The first book will be oriented toward encouraging accomplishments; the second, toward nurturing feelings and stressing the bond between parent and child. The first book will give practical solutions, with plenty of do's and don'ts, while the second will offer suggestions for how to encourage a child's development according to his own readiness. The first book will chart child development by the week and by the month; the second will tell us about general tendencies, approximate age levels, and general phases in the growing years. Frequently, the first book will have been written by a pediatrician, and the second by a specialist in child development. And more often than not, the first book will have been written by a man, and the second by a woman, usually a mother.

Better the child should cry than the father.

German proverb

"Speak roughly to your little boy,
And beat him when he sneezes:
He does it only to annoy,
Because he knows it teases."

Lewis Carroll (1865)

"Oh, that a mother would take common sense,
not custom, as her guide."

Mary R. Melendy, M.D., Ph.D. (1911)

"For years we have given scientific attention to the
care and rearing of plants and animals, but we have
allowed babies to be raised chiefly by tradition."

Edith Belle Lowry (1912)

"There is a sensible way of treating children.
Treat them as if they were young adults. . . .
Never hug and kiss them, never let them sit in your
lap. . . . Try it out. In a week's time you will find
how easy it is to be perfectly objective with your
child and at the same time kindly. You will be
utterly ashamed of the mawkish, sentimental way
you have been handling it."

John B. Watson (1928)

Chapter 3

Understanding Basic Parenting Differences

Raising children presents us with a nearly endless variety of situations to respond to, and the differences between men's and women's ways of feeling and reasoning come into play as we do so. Among the most debated child-rearing issues in our society are breast-feeding and weaning, how to interpret crying, whether children should sleep with their parents, and when and how children should separate from their mothers. Let us now look at these issues from points of view that reflect characteristically male and female responses.

BREAST-FEEDING

Many men in our culture tend to think of breast-feeding solely as a means of providing food. After all, that is what the term breast-feeding implies. Also, most child-rearing books talk about breast-feeding only as a way of providing nourishment, not nurturing. When a baby cries, her father is likely to pick the child up and say to the mother, "Jennifer is hungry." If the baby cries again half an hour later, he will often wonder why she is "hungry again."

Since they generally believe that breast-feeding is only about food, and this food source is tied up with the mother, many men see breast-feeding as dependency. And since they tend to view dependency as a negative thing, it seems best to them that a child be weaned sooner rather than later. This is said so often and by so many authoritative voices that many mothers actually end up believing it, even though on a deeper level it may not feel right to them. Only very recently have mothers been encouraged to nurse for longer than a few weeks—and even so, this advice is usually based on the nutritional and health-giving properties of breast milk, not on the emotional and psychological advantages of breast-feeding. But to most nursing women, breast-feeding does not only mean feeding; it means nurturing, comforting, fulfilling a need for closeness, and soothing feelings of fear, loneliness, or boredom. In fact, breast-*nurturing* is a much better term for it than breast-*feeding* is.

Barton D. Schmitt, M.D., states that if a breast-feeding mother does not separate the times she holds a child for comfort from the times she nurses for feeding, the child will learn to eat whenever she is upset and the mother may become an "indispensible mother."[1] In other words, the child will fail to become independent. These ideas, though fallacious, are nonetheless thoroughly ingrained in many men—and some women, too. They reflect a characteristically male point of view, but they ignore the fact that a child will not nurse once she no longer needs or wants to do so. There are numerous cultures in which mothers nurse frequently, and without much thought, whenever their children want. In due time, these children *all* wean and become, we may assume, quite independent adults.

Then, too, the vast majority of women do not breast-feed because they enjoy having someone dependent on them, but because it fulfills a mother's basic emotional need to be suckled by her child and to feel the child's presence in her arms and against her body. In fact, the long-term nursing mother is simply enjoying intimacy and bonding with her child. A mother who feels a great loss when her child weans, especially if the child weans early, is often looked upon as emotionally dependent on the child. In reality, she is grieving over the break in her intimate connection with her child, which is based not on dependency but on maternal emotions.

My first child, Yvonne, was nursing about four times a day when she abruptly and totally weaned herself. No amount of coaxing, even when she was groggy with sleep, made her latch on again. When it became clear that Yvonne had definitely stopped nursing, I felt I had lost something precious. It had been so sudden. Other people, who did not understand the situation, told me, "You are much too hung up on her. You should be pleased that she is independent now." How could I explain that her independence and our intimacy were totally unrelated as far as I was concerned?

CRYING

Since men generally believe that the purpose of communication is to give or receive information, they tend to see a baby's crying as an attempt on the baby's part to convey information, to indicate that something is wrong. To help new parents, many male-authored child-rearing books provide lists of possible problems to look for when a baby is crying—an open diaper pin, a wet diaper, being too hot or too cold, hunger, or pain. Emotional needs, or the need for touching, being held, or experiencing motion are not usually on the checklist, because they can't be seen or measured. If none of the problems fits and the list is exhausted, these books will say there is probably no "real" reason the baby is crying; it means only that she wants to be held, which offers an excellent opportunity for the baby to learn to be autonomous and to soothe herself.

From many a woman's point of view, however, talk is for establishing connections, so a baby's crying may indicate a need for human interaction. Mothers usually see nothing wrong with responding to and carrying on interaction with their children, because interaction means connectedness and intimacy, which women are naturally inclined to.

Much has been said about crying. In the first half of the twentieth century, crying was viewed as manipulative behavior by the infant. Mothers were told that if they answered their babies' cries, the children would become spoiled because they would learn that crying would get them what they wanted. A child whose every cry is answered will become the household tyrant, warned a pamphlet produced by the United States Children's Bureau in 1926. This advice may have been, in part, a reaction to the practices of the 1800s, when children were often overfed and drugged to keep them quiet.[2] In any case, it was heavily promoted by the experts of the time, such as Dr. John B. Watson and Mrs. Max West, whose nationally acclaimed manual on infant care stressed that crying babies should be checked for physical problems and then left to cry themselves to sleep.

In the meantime, research continued to try to establish, in detail, the meaning of a baby's cry. As a product of this research, three basic cries are often mentioned: the hunger cry, the anger cry, and the pain cry. The many facets of babies' crying—when they cry, for how long, when they stop and under what conditions, and so on—have all been duly studied. Scientific curiosity apparently knows no bounds when it comes to the crying baby.

Today, many people believe that crying is a mechanism designed to serve as a signal to the mother that her infant requires attention. Crying is therefore classified, in the language of anthropology, as an attachment and survival behavior, because it serves to bring mother and baby together. (Despite the belief that crying signals a need for attention, however, many child-rearing experts nevertheless instruct parents that it is up to *them* to determine whether a particular cry needs to be answered or not).

Desmond Morris once wrote that a baby's cry means, "Please come," and the smile means, "Please stay." This interpretation, however, is foreign to mothers who have continual contact with their infants. For crying to mean "come here," mother and baby would have to be in different places, but mothers who practice intimate and connected child rearing are with their babies most of the time. The idea that crying is a survival mechanism to alert the mother is probably purely a modern-day concept, developed and supported by people who assume that separation between mothers and children is the norm. They assume this because it reflects a characteristically male point of view toward issues of intimacy of independence, and, as we have seen, male values are the ones that tend to dominate in our society. But looked at from a characteristically female perspective, as most mothers can tell you, what crying really means is that something is wrong.

One male researcher even suggested that the word "mama"—the beginning of language for most babies—is an outgrowth of an infant's crying and whimpering for her mother. This is totally contrary to my experience. Both of my children, by the age of six months, would often sit contentedly in the backpack carrier and say "mamamamam" over and over again. It seems obvious to me that the word is merely the mouthing action of a breast-feeding baby with vocalization behind it. The seemingly meaningless "mamamamam" eventually becomes "mama" and "numnum," a "secret" word for breast-nurturing used by many toddlers. In fact, some form of the sound "ma," usually repeated, is the basis for the informal word for mother (the word that children use, the equivalent of "mama" or "mommy" in English) in virtually every language in the world.[3]

In our society, crying babies are a given. It should be noted, however, that virtually all of the studies that have been done on the subject also assume that babies are, as a matter of course, frequently separated from their mothers. But when we study mothers who routinely carry their infants for most of the day and sleep with them at night, we find that *their* babies cry most when they are not being carried (excluding crying brought about by pain, allergies, or "unexplainable reasons" [also known as colic]). This simple observation should make us wonder why it is that we separate babies so much from their mothers, rather than debating whether or how long to let babies cry. If separation so often results in crying and connectedness in contentment, why did we ever start separating babies from mothers? And why are we doing all of this research on the best ways to deal with something that can be prevented in the first place? (I also find it amazing that researchers can sit by, with pen, paper, and stopwatch in hand, and observe a crying child, rather than being moved by empathy to do something to help.)

A group of mothers summed up the difference between men's and women's responses to a child's crying by saying, "When baby fusses, dads think there is something physically wrong, while moms tend to think it is something emotional." It is not that men lack the desire to soothe their children, but they tend to look at a crying baby as a problem to which they must find an answer. Who has not seen a father try desperately to figure out why his child is crying, only to hand the baby to his wife in frustration and say, "I don't know what's the matter with her. You figure it out." To him, the baby's crying meant, "I'm trying to tell you that something is hurting me." To a mother, a baby's crying can also mean, "I'm lonely. Be with me. Connect with me. Interact with me."

One parenting educator told me that "let them cry" is one of the greatest sources of conflict between mothers and fathers. If parents understand each other's feelings and appreciate the differences between them, they can instead observe their child to determine what is best for *her* in a particular situation. As with so many decisions in parenting, there is frequently a delicate balance. We have to decide when nurturing becomes overprotection, and when enforced independence becomes excessive stress. We are constantly gauging and weighing our choices, and sometimes we make mistakes. But it can give us greater peace of mind to know that at times, we are choosing not between right and wrong, but male and female. In the case of crying, it is my unwavering belief that the cry of an infant or young child must *never* go unanswered.

HOLDING

Caring for others is an integral part of the drive for intimacy and connectedness, and thus a strong female trait. An intimate part of caring is touching, caressing, and holding. In general, women thrive on closeness, especially with loved ones, and most of all with their own children; their desire for physical contact with their children is usually stronger than that of men. The pleasure and ease with which most women hold babies and children is likely a natural outgrowth of breast-nurturing. A woman will often hold a baby for intimacy's sake, because it simply feels good to both of them.

To men, holding tends to look like encouraging dependency, which, if carried on for "too long," is not good for a child. Men usually prefer more distance, more frequently. "The need to control distance with others seems to be a universal male trait," writes Cris Evatt.[4] A man will usually hold a baby for the baby's sake—when she needs to be held—rather than for the pleasure of holding the child.

One male doctor advises that if you hold your baby too much, she will gradually forget how to amuse herself, feel bored, deserted, and miserable when left alone, and cry for attention.[5] This doctor most likely did not recognize how his own male gender characteristics may have been at work here. Instead of realizing why he was making the statement, he looked for a plausible explanation for why babies should not spend too much time in their mothers' arms. To him, there were real pitfalls for a baby who is held too much. Numerous other books also give mothers advice on how they can make sure their babies learn to amuse themselves. But this ignores the fact that babies were never meant to "amuse themselves" to begin with. First of all, babies—who, as we all know, cannot take care of themselves—obviously aren't meant to be *by* themselves. Second, babies don't need to be *amused* at all, if they are simply held.

When I was pregnant with my first child, I often wondered what I should do to entertain her once she was born. I couldn't begin to remember all the "ways to stimulate your child" listed in the child-rearing books. Later, I realized that babies need not be entertained in order not to be bored. Babies easily get all the stimulation they need just by being included in daily activities, either by being carried around or placed close to the family. We don't need to do anything special, only involve them.

And when we involve them, they don't need all the educational toys or stuffed animals to play with so that they can "amuse themselves." Before the mass marketing of elaborate (and often not very interesting) toys for babies, children were carried by their mothers and passively participated in all of their daily activities, whether shopping, chopping wood, cooking, dancing, or walking. More and more mothers are carrying their babies again today, in a sling or a backpack, as they shop, do housework, or work at a home computer (although the latter can be more difficult since a baby can get restless if her mother sits quietly for too long). Children of all ages like action. Every parent knows that babies, especially, find motion to be very soothing. Lack of motion can produce tension in a young child, which must be relieved through motion. Forcing a child to sit or lie by herself at a very early age can make her frustrated and bored because she is then called on to produce action for herself that she may be too young to accomplish. What young children really need is to feel included and connected in life.

The major justification offered, usually by men, for forcing children to be by themselves is that unless they are taught independence, they will become incapable of being by themselves. But it has been observed by researchers that babies who are carried routinely during their first year are often quite content to be put down, and turn happily to exploration and play activities, as they get older.[6] Many mothers know this. There is no need to fear, as some experts claim, that babies who are held "too much" (that is, babies who experience routine in-arms connectedness with their mothers) will not learn to amuse themselves and as a result will become overly dependent on their mother's care.

Let me give a word of caution, though, about mentioning an age together with an expected accomplishment. I have never liked the idea of saying that a child should be able to do a particular thing at a particular time. This can create unrealistic expectations that set the stage for frustration and conflict. If a book suggests that a child *should* be able to stay with a babysitter by the age of three years, some parents may start to think there is something wrong with their child if she is three years and three months old but still cries when left with a babysitter. Children vary too much, both in personality and in growth patterns, for a one-age-fits-all approach. My own two children, Yvonne and Michelle, are two years apart in age. Yvonne quit nursing abruptly at one year of age; Michelle nursed until she was over four. Yet on the babysitter issue, they were strikingly similar. I first left each of them with a babysitter some time during her second year. I would leave after she was asleep, although she knew I'd be going out. Some time during her third year, I would tell her when I was going out for the evening and allow her to choose whether the babysitter, Sharon, or I would put her to bed. Both of them decided, at some point between the ages of three and three and a half, that it would be fine if Sharon read her a story, rubbed her back, and lay down with her until she fell asleep. We must always keep in mind that all children are individuals, and it is the role of the parent to be aware of each child's readiness for new experiences, as well as to recognize, accept, and speak up for the child who does not seem to be ready.

We know that babies who are routinely carried cry much less than those who follow the now-traditional Western pattern of early and frequent separation. More than once, during La Leche League conventions (where over 1,000 parents and babies may be in attendance), hotel personnel have been heard to say, "With all those babies, it is amazing that there is so little crying." La Leche League mothers routinely carry their babies, so instead of having to rely on crying to bring a response and establish communication, these in-arms babies develop very adequate yet less stressful signals.[7] An in-arms baby who is breast-fed is also less likely to cry for any length of time, because her cry stimulates a hormonal response in her mother that causes her breasts to fill with milk. This full feeling triggers in the mother the desire for relief from milk tension as well as the desire to suckle the child.[8] The child is nursed, stops crying, and becomes content.

Researchers have learned that motion and the sound of the human heartbeat—both of which are inextricably entwined with holding and breast nurturing—soothe babies. This has given rise to products ranging from automatic baby swings to pacifiers. Enterprising companies are now even marketing audiocassette tapes to soothe and quiet babies "just like mother." As one doctor I know exclaimed, "Well, eureka! Why don't we just use mother?"

WEANING

Since men in our culture tend to think of breast-feeding as dependent behavior, they are likely to advocate enforced weaning, usually at a specific predetermined age, and they often prescribe schedules and timetables for accomplishing it. I focus on weaning from the breast here, but men's attitudes toward weaning—whether from the breast or the bottle—tend to be governed by the same concern: the issue of encouraging independence and discouraging dependency.

Asked why weaning is important, Lee Salk, Ph.D., replied that it is one of the first steps toward a child's independence.[9] Further, he said, some mothers seek to delay weaning because they enjoy having their children dependent on them. In effect, he criticized the long-term nursing mother for being selfish, and blamed her for being unhealthily dependent on her child.

To most women, however, breast-nurturing is an act of intimate communication between mother and child. Mothers see breast-feeding not only as a means of providing their babies with nourishment, but also as a means to comfort, interact, bond, and communicate with their children in a nonverbal way. Since, from the mother's point of view, breast-feeding or breast-nurturing does not mean holding a child back, weaning is not something that needs to be forced on a child so that she will develop independence. It is simply a process that occurs as the child's horizons expand and sucking at the breast is no longer necessary. Virginia Pomeranz, M.D., author of *The First Five Years*, writes on the issue of weaning from a characteristically female point of view: "I would say that [a mother] should nurse as long as both she and the baby enjoy it."[10] La Leche League's manual, *The Womanly Art of Breastfeeding*, says that weaning is just another step in growing up. "What is there to be gained by putting an end to this wonderful relationship?" its authors ask.[11]

The very word "weaning" is rather interesting in that, over time, its definition has come to reflect precisely the experience our modern society expects children to have when they stop nursing. Although it has its root in the Anglo-Saxon *awenian*, meaning to *accustom a child to the loss* of mother's milk, its current accepted meaning is *withdrawing by substituting something else*.

In our individualistic society, we expect children to learn at a very early age to get nourishment from another source than the breast, and to find comfort in something other than a human being—pacifiers, teddy bears, blankets. But a mother who allows her child total intimacy and connectedness during the early years, and allows a gradual weaning process to take place when the child initiates it, will rarely find that her child has to learn to accept a substitute. Children who naturally wean from the breast do not usually seek substitutes at all; they simply move on from one source of nourishment to the next, enlarging their horizons as they move from breast-feeding to eating other foods, from needing intense physical intimacy with mother to no longer having a need for that particular closeness. Likewise, a child who "weans" from seeking intimacy with her mother during times of stress to being able to handle stress on her own does not usually do so by using a substitute—a blanket or a teddy bear—but simply moves on from one source to another, to her father, siblings, friends, or someone else with whom she feels comfortable—and eventually to herself. This is not something children need to be taught or trained to do; they do it naturally as they become more independent.

A child who resists enforced weaning is displaying a perfectly normal biological reaction. She is simply not ready to break the intimate bond with her mother. This reaction is so normal—and, because so few children are allowed to wean naturally, so prevalent in our society— that the term "separation anxiety" was coined by psychoanalysts to describe this disturbing reaction. The stronger a young child's attachment to her parents, the greater her distress and even panic is likely to be when she is separated from her parents and left with a stranger or left alone. But these distress signals are signs of love and loss, not of wanting to control or be controlled, nor of an unhealthy dependency, writes Selma Fraiberg, professor of child psychoanalysis at the University of Michigan Medical Center, in *Every Child's Birthright*.[12] And the answer is simple. "Our own motherly instincts tell us the remedy," write the mothers in *The Womanly Art of Breastfeeding*. "Avoid the separation until he is ready for it. Saves wear and tear on everybody." That wonderfully simple advice, testimony to mothers' inherent tendency toward intimacy and connectedness, easily outshines the volumes of scientific research that "prove1 the same thing.

It is important to realize, too, that even though breast-nurturing is a wonderful thing for children, there comes a time when neither the breast nor a substitute is needed or wanted. Dependency on the mother for breast-nurturing or intimacy lasts only as long as the need is there. In fact, mothers who have allowed their children a full in-arms experience and natural weaning are known to comment on the delightful spirit and *independence* of their children. No wonder. Eating is wonderful, too, and feeling full may be gratifying, but when we've had enough we can content-edly walk away from the table. In the same way, when a child has had enough intimacy from her mother, she can contentedly move away from her. And a mother who has experienced full intimacy with her baby is usually able, willing, and happy to allow the child to reach out for independence. Her needs have been met, too. This is true of most mothers, whether breast- or bottle-feeding, who practice connected child-rearing and allow child-led weaning.

SLEEPING ARRANGEMENTS

There is probably not a single family in the Western world that has not had some conflict over whether a child should be permitted to sleep in her parents' bed, at least on occa-sion. Very young children, and children of any age who are frightened or under stress, often express a desire to sleep with their parents. Yet this remains one of the strong-est child-rearing taboos in our culture. Many child-care experts approach the subject with something like a mis-sionary fervor, and a great many of them agree: Never, no matter what the circumstances, should a child be permit-ted to share a bed with a parent, and certainly not on a permanent basis. Almost always, such an arrangement is described as "unhealthy."

The health issue most often referred to is, of course, the development of the child's independence. But this, as we have seen, reflects a characteristically male concept of what health is; for men, independence feels healthy. But for women, intimacy and connectedness with their young children feels healthy, and this is promoted by having the children sleep with them. Many women find it feels especially healthy, and comfortable, to breast-feed when lying down at night. They also feel better, and usually sleep better, when they have a constant awareness of their babies' well-being. In many cultures, particularly societies where child-rearing expertise is considered a woman's specialty, it would be considered unhealthy for babies to sleep *without* their mothers.

An article on co-family sleeping research conducted by Deborah Madansky, M.D., and Craig Edelbrock, Ph.D., of the University of Massachusetts Medical School, stated that "frequent co-sleeping is closely intertwined with child sleep problems."[13] But this is far from the objective scientific finding that it may seem to be. Upon closer examination, we learn that the "problems" referred to are that frequent co-sleepers are more likely to resist sleeping alone, to want someone with them while going to sleep, and to wake up more often during the night seeking companionship. In other words, these researchers have defined a "problem" as anything that deviates from the entrenched, essentially male, belief that children *should* be alone in their own beds at night. The writers never consider whether this "problem" behavior is based on natural needs or not.

A mother I know told me that her four-year-old was afraid to sleep by himself because he saw shadows on the wall that he thought were ghosts. So her husband came up with what was, he felt, a super idea to help his son get rid of his fears. The father made a great to-do about "hiring" some "ghostbusters" to take the shadows away. The father became enthusiastically involved in trying to impress upon his son that the ghostbusters were successful. Unfortunately, the child was not impressed; the shadows were still there afterwards. "I think he really wants to sleep with us," the child's mother told me. "What do you think?" I agreed with her. Her husband's idea was certainly creative and might have worked. It was a worthwhile experiment. But when the child remained afraid of the shadows, his father felt rejected, disgusted, and angry, and still could not accept his wife's opinion. "This kid is four years old!" he exclaimed.

As if the conflict between independence and intimacy were not enough, another health issue has recently been raised to discourage parents from sleeping with their children. In 1991, New York State Attorney General Robert Abrams and the American Academy of Pediatrics requested that a hangtag be placed on all mattresses, reading: "Suffocation warning. Never place a child on a mattress. They may suffocate there." Articles have appeared in major publications warning parents not to let their children sleep in their beds because of the danger of suffocation, or of their parents rolling over on them and killing them.

What this plays on is every parent's nightmare, Sudden Infant Death Syndrome (SIDS). Much research has been done to try to determine the cause or causes of SIDS, but to date none has found and the tragedy continues to baffle researchers. There is no conclusive evidence that mattresses have anything to do with it. In fact, new research indicates that having a young child sleep with her mother may actually help to *prevent* SIDS.[14] There are several theories as to why this might be so, including the possibility that hearing and feeling the heartbeat and breathing of the mother helps the baby to breathe in rhythm with her, or that a mother sleeping beside her child will instantly know of and react to any changes in the child's breathing. In any case, it does seem likely that sleeping together, staying in constant close contact, may in fact help reduce the likelihood of SIDS.

The mattress warning seems to me rather like saying that, since some children have died in traffic accidents, all cars should bear the message: "Never place a baby in a car. If an accident occurs, she may die there." Of course, such a warning would be unthinkable in our culture, where transportation by car is accepted as a norm. Instead, research has been done to develop safe child seats, and laws have been passed requiring children to ride in them. If the need for bonding and intimacy between mother and child were as much an institution in our society as car travel is, we would probably see research into the safest possible ways for babies to sleep with their parents, rather than warnings on mattresses. As James McKenna, Ph.D., professor of anthropology and adjunct assistant professor in the Department of Psychiatry and Neurology at the University of California's Irvine School of Medicine, said in an article on SIDS research, "Scientists bring to their work their own experiences and world views. Most likely neither SIDS researchers nor sleep investigators slept with their own parents. And most certainly the majority of today's scientists have been socialized in a culture that regards parent-infant co-sleeping as unnatural and dangerous."[15] One wonders if, had the Attorney General and most of the members of the American Academy of Pediatrics been mothers who had nursed and slept with their babies, they would have come up with the same advice.

ENFORCED SEPARATION

Enforced separation takes many forms in most children's lives. Often, it comes in the shape of one of the child-rearing issues discussed above, such as weaning, holding, and sleeping arrangements. But because forcing children to be and do as much on their own as possible is such a recurrent theme in Western child-rearing advice, the practice deserves some consideration on *its* own.

Many child-rearing books, particularly ones written by men, are essentially manuals for enforcing separation, complete with schedules and instructions for each new separation to be introduced. This approach to raising children fits in well with not one but several male gender characteristics. The first, obviously, is the need for independence. Men tend to view attachment to the mother as dependence on the mother. Dependence is not desirable, so attachment also is not desirable; consequently, separation must be good. Also, as we saw in the previous chapter, most men feel comfortable with clearly defined hierarchies and rules. Many therefore relate well to detailed and explicit schedules and lists of do's and don'ts for child rearing.

Women, on the other hand, are usually far less inclined to interpret attachment as dependence, and even if they do, they don't see dependence as necessarily bad, especially for young children. Since they place a greater value on interdependence, they don't necessarily feel they've "lost" some kind of battle if their children want to nurse or crawl into bed with them. (See The Competing Reasons for Separation and Intimacy, page 68.)

But is it possible to set aside our gender-based assumptions and instead focus on the way separation, particularly enforced separation, actually affects children?

A great volume of research, starting over fifty years ago with the work of such researchers as Anna Freud, has confirmed that a child needs to form a trusting relationship with her primary caretaker, usually a mother or mother substitute.[16] This trusting relationship develops when a child experiences total intimacy with her mother from birth, which teaches an infant that mother can be relied on to be there when her baby needs her. This is followed in due time by gradual, child-guided weaning, and enlargement of the child's world to include father, siblings, and friends.

A trusting relationship can be undermined by early separation of the child from her mother, particularly at certain ages. "We have sufficient clinical evidence," writes Humberto Nagera, Ph.D., professor of psychology at the University of Montana, "to assume that, though separations from his biological object [mother or primary caretaker] are always unwelcome to the very young infant, there is a particularly vulnerable and critical period in this regard in the early part of the second year of life. When the child is confronted with the mother's absence, his automatic response is an anxiety state that on many occasions reaches overwhelming proportions. Repeated traumas of this type in especially susceptible children will not fail to have serious consequences for their later development."[17] As to how to determine which children are "especially susceptible," however, Dr. Nagera admits this is virtually impossible to do until later, when they start to show the results of too much stress in their younger years. At that point, it's too late to prevent it.

Most young children cannot easily handle separation without experiencing stress. In *The Hurried Child*, David Elkind writes that the more we demand that our children grow up in a hurry—wean themselves, handle aloneness, carry emotional and psychological burdens for which they are not ready—the more likely it is that they will be overstressed.[18] "Modern mothering," write Anne Moir and David Jessel, "a result of social, political, and economic pressure on the woman to play a fuller part in the world, may provoke signals of infant stress resulting from environmental demands which are alien to [their] biological

The Competing Reasons
for Separation and Intimacy

What are the reasons most often given by men and women for enforcing independence and separation? What are the most common reasons for allowing a child full and total access to her parents until she develops independence on her own?

Men who favor enforced independence say:

- *Maturity depends on the ability to be independent and self-reliant.*
- *Independence is a way of life in our society, and must therefore be taught as early as possible.*
- *Independence is necessary for individual identity awareness, especially for boys.*
- *Separation is necessary to reduce the threat of dependence (intimacy) between male babies and their mothers.*
- *Independence raises a baby's self-esteem.*
- *Independence will only be learned well if taught from infancy on.*

Women who favor enforced independence say:

- *Mothers need their sleep and some quiet time themselves.*
- *The family will benefit if a baby learns to comfort herself.*
- *It causes less fuss when a baby or child learns to be self-reliant and can be separated from mother for some predetermined period of time.*
- *Separation is beneficial for children because it encourages self-reliance.*
- *Separation means fewer demands on a mother's time and energy, especially if she works outside the home.*
- *It keeps everyone (doctor, husband, "authorities") happy if a family conforms to "standard" child-rearing practices. The doctor, or the family, or our friends might consider me a bad mother if we didn't.*
- *Independence must be taught and, if necessary, forced upon a child.*

Men who favor allowing a child free access to intimacy say:	Women who favor allowing a child free access to intimacy say:
• Mother-child bonding is necessary, and is better accomplished when separation is not forced.	• It fulfills a mother's innate desire to connect and be intimate with her child.
• Early child rearing is mainly a woman's domain. Mothers should do what feels right for them.	• The relationship between a mother and her child is based on connectedness, not on separation.
• It makes mothers happier.	• Mothers feel threatened by the idea of forcing separation too early because they empathize with their babies.
• It makes babies happier.	
• A child will become independent without training, once she has outgrown the dependency stage.	• Mothers and children thrive on intimacy.
	• It makes babies happier.
	• It makes mothers happier.

People who favor allowing a child free access to intimacy tend to focus their arguments on the needs of the child and the mother-child relationship; basically, connectedness and intimacy make children happy. The main reason many women do not want to be separated from their young children, they say, is simply that both thrive on the intimacy.

The arguments of those who advocate teaching separation tend to focus on the opinions and needs of other people—the family or outside authorities. I have never found it claimed that mother and child thrive on enforced separation—only that it is, in some abstract way, better for baby and easier for the mother and family. Whether it creates mutual happiness is rarely discussed.

needs."[19] And separation need not be especially lengthy to be stressful. To a very young child, time is meaningless. The anxiety of separation fills the whole moment, and the moment is without end because she has no concept of half an hour, a few hours, or one day.

Stress is not always a negative thing, of course. It can make us do something to improve a situation. It can even be exciting. But it can also have serious adverse effects, and young children are more likely to suffer from them. Adults have a far greater capacity to handle stress and/or to do something about its source. Young children simply have not developed the resources to recognize, express, or deal with stress for what it is, so they must rely on their parents to interpret what is going on. But if a child is experiencing stress as a result of separation that is being forced on her *by* her parents, her reaction is unlikely to be interpreted accurately. After all, the parents are proceeding from the assumption that the separation is a positive thing. They may even think, by extension, that the stress reaction itself is a positive thing. This makes it difficult for them to truly empathize with their child, for whom the experience is anything but positive.

From the child's perspective, it can be extremely stressful to be left with strangers, to have to handle night fears alone, or to have to handle any type of separation from her source of comfort prematurely. Many children suffer such great stress in trying to adjust to manipulated separation that they become the troubled children clinicians are so familiar with, according to Elkind.[20] I know of one family who took their three-year-old daughter to a psychiatrist because she could not handle the stress of nighttime separation. They apparently saw this as the expression of an emotional problem, rather than of an emotional need. Meanwhile, the parents down the street were taking their teenage son to another psychiatrist because he was failing in school and taking drugs, problems the doctor concluded were largely due to the stress he had experienced as a child forced to grow up too soon. Many older children suffer from less severe, but no less real, stress-related problems. Often these are the same kinds of complaints that have long been recognized as the product of stress in adults: headaches, stomach problems, depression, hyperactivity, and lethargy.

As Selma Fraiberg, a self-described children's advocate, writes, "If we generalize at all, we can say that . . . all children at all ages need stability, continuity, and predictability in their human partnership for the fullest realization of their potential for love, for trust, for learning and self worth."[21] We may not always like the fact that infants and young children need us as much as they do, and we may not always be able to give them what they need. But this cannot erase the fact that a child needs to form a close, intimate relationship with her mother from birth, and that anything less may have a negative effect on her emotional development. Similarly, we may not like the fact that a child is afraid of the dark, does not want to go to sleep by herself, does not want to stay with babysitters, is afraid to go to the dentist by herself, or does not want to wean yet. But we must not let ourselves confuse our preferences with her needs. As one father told me, "I've discovered that when I do something strictly for my benefit or to fulfill my need, I inevitably shortchange someone else."

GAINING PERSPECTIVE

How do we know, then, when a child is ready to be left with a babysitter, to sleep alone, to wean, or to go away to camp? Listen to the child. And reflect on the mother's feelings and input, especially when the child is an infant. Generally, it's time when a little push and encouragement do not result in a major traumatic reaction.

Throughout history and throughout the world, different societies and cultures have dealt with child rearing in conspicuously different ways. Virtually unique to our Western culture are an extensive separation of mothers from their children and an emphasis on training children to be independent (the Japanese, by contrast, believe that an infant at birth is a separate creature whose primary task is to learn connectedness and to become part of the group).[22] The prominence of male child-rearing experts is also virtually unique to our culture. The emphasis on separation and independence comes up again and again as one studies the way we raise our children, which is hardly surprising given that independence and individualism are characteristically male concerns. Historically and globally, though, the raising of children, especially babies, has been primarily a female arena. It is my hope, and indeed my belief, that coming generations will learn to celebrate the uniqueness and contributions of both men and women, and welcome the return of children to the bosom of the family.

"Babies should be trained from their earliest days to sleep regularly and should never be awoken in the night for feeding. . . . Baby should be given his own bedroom from the very beginning. He should never be brought into the living room at night."

The Motherhood Book (1935)

"You know more than you think you do. . . . Don't be afraid to trust your own common sense. Bringing up your child won't be a complicated job if you take it easy, trust your own instincts, and follow the directions that your doctor gives you."

Benjamin Spock, M.D. (1945)

Chapter 4

Reading the Experts

If you ask a woman who the primary caretakers of children are, she will answer, "Women." (This is true. Even in cultures where men have been encouraged to share in housework and child rearing, such as the United States and Sweden, mothers generally spend far more of their time on mothering than fathers spend on fathering—even when both hold full-time jobs outside the home.) If you ask the same woman whether men and women differ in their approaches to child rearing, she will say, without hesitation, "Yes." If you ask her who the expert advice on child rearing comes from, she will answer, "Men." And then her face will light up and she'll say, "I've never thought of that. Why *is* that?"

It's a good question. Why is it that the child-rearing agendas of men have been so successfully implemented in our society in the last century or so, even though the approach so often runs contrary to the feelings of women, who do most of the child care? To find the answer, we must take a brief look at history.

Prior to the beginning of the industrial revolution, which started in the 1800s, babies were born at home and breast-fed for an extended period of time. Two years was not unusual. Young children slept with or close to their mothers or wet nurses and were taken care of by them or by other members of the (usually extended) family. What education they received came from members of the household. Not much special fuss was made over them. Their real importance to the family would not begin until they became contributing members of the group. Children were regarded not as miniature adults, but as children, with children's needs and abilities. Their dependence on adults was accepted as natural. A gradual process of separation took place through a transition period that involved weaning from the breast, weaning from the family bed and mother's arms, and weaning from the tie with mother, until the child became an independent young adult, ready to participate in the family's daily activities.

THE RISE OF THE OUTSIDE EXPERT

With the coming of the industrial revolution, tremendous changes began to take place. The extended family began to splinter into small nuclear families, as parts of the family moved away from each other to be nearer to employment. Fathers, and sometimes mothers and other family members, were working in factories and absent from the household for extended periods of time every day. While in the past young mothers had learned the art of mothering from their own mothers or other members of the older generation, they were now much more isolated. This created a sizeable market for written sources of information about child rearing. Since at the time men were the scholars and researchers, it was mainly men who began to write the books on the latest scientific discoveries and opinions, including the ones on the care of children.

Naturally, men were inclined to have different ideas about child rearing than women had had, particularly in the area of promoting independence in children. We can imagine, however, that these new theories were not without appeal to the women of the time. While mothers had previously had other household members to help them rear their children and do all of the other tasks in the home, these responsibilities now fell on mothers alone. Therefore, the more the children could do for themselves, the less stress there was on mothers.

The many inventions that followed to help ease their situation were doubtless also welcomed by mothers struggling to attend to children and housekeeping by themselves. In the past, wet nurses had been available only to the wealthy. Now, mass-produced mother substitutes—bottles for formula feeding, pacifiers, carriages and strollers, cribs, playpens—began to become available to most mothers, relieving them of some of their burdens. The period of the baby's dependence on his mother was reduced, and their intimate togetherness was reduced along with it. There was less breast-feeding and close contact between mothers and babies.

The inventions that separated children from their mothers for the sake of convenience came with the approval of the male experts, who emphasized that independence and autonomy in a child were desirable and good. In turn, bottle-feeding meant that mothers, who no longer felt the hormone-induced heaviness in their breasts when their children cried, could more easily follow the experts' advice, because their physical desire to pick up and nurse their children was subdued. The downward spiral in mother-child intimacy, aided by a reduction in the hormones that promote a woman's mothering behavior, allowed mothers to accept an outsider's point of view more readily and, as a result, to separate themselves from their babies even more. In other words, industrialization split families and isolated women; overwhelmed mothers benefitted from having less dependent children; inventors created devices to help reduce the burdens on mothers, and in the process hastened the return to a prepregnancy and prelactating state; and the research and opinions of male experts, whose ideas were formed within the framework of their own gender characteristics, not only approved of this but encouraged ever more separation and earlier enforced independence.

Other factors came into play as well. In the 1800s, the rise of scientific theory was turning the practice of medicine from an art into a science, and practitioners were seeking to expand their influence. One way they did this was by turning their attention to pregnancy, childbirth, and child rearing, which had previously been considered normal (if occasionally dangerous) parts of domestic life. To make these processes into things requiring a doctor's advice or intervention, doctors promoted the view that they were, in fact, medical problems. Over time, this effort was largely successful, leading to the near-disappearance of midwifery in the United States and even laws in some states prohibiting women from intentionally giving birth at home.

At the same time, researchers were pursuing the study of education as a science in its own right, and they began to take note of children's educability and potential for molding. An all-out effort was begun to educate children for adulthood, led, once again, primarily by male researchers and educators. In a paper entitled "Medical Advice on Child Rearing 1550-1900," Alice Judson Ryerson, Ph.D., of the Harvard Graduate School of Education, points out that there may have been a link between the interest in early independence training and the desire to mold a personality that could function effectively in an industrial society.[1] Thus, advice on child rearing no longer came from inside the family or female-based tradition, but from the outside, and was geared toward the needs of the male-oriented scientific and industrial world.

The encouragement of early independence also coincided with and was reinforced by a religious and philosophical climate that included the Methodist movement, led by John Wesley. Wesley's message was that Christian perfection and personal communion with God depended on self-reliance, a quality best achieved by early independence training. David McClelland, author of *The Achieving Society*, who is cited by Dr. Ryerson, feels that the strength of the movement could have been sufficient to cause changes in general child-rearing patterns.[2]

MISPLACED RITES OF PASSAGE

Other changes that resulted from the fragmented nature of industrial society also had an effect on child-rearing practices. Previously, babies had been carried by their mothers (or placed in close proximity to where they were working), were breast-fed when necessary, and slept next to or close by their mothers at night. A girl child, as she weaned from her mother's breast, remained nevertheless close to her mother, developing her own female identity and need for connectedness and intimacy. Then, as now, she underwent a sort of natural initiation rite into adulthood as she matured, through the onset of menstruation. Even though it is often considered a nuisance and efforts are made to pretend it does not occur, womanhood still happens naturally to girls.

For boys, there is no such natural initiation experience to signal the beginning of manhood. Therefore, in most societies, some kind of formal recognition of the transition to adult status takes place when the boy is deemed ready to leave the intimate female world and become part of the adult male world. This is not necessarily the kind of grueling experience or painful physical testing customary in some preliterate cultures. In our society, for instance, one rite of passage used to occur when boys went from wearing short pants and knickers to wearing long pants. The important thing was that a boy publicly left childhood behind, breaking the tie of dependency and intimacy with his mother in a way that was recognizable and gave him a sense of pride and independence, the building blocks of his male identity.

But the social upheaval brought about by the industrial revolution ultimately put an end to these rites of passage, and no others have developed to take their place. As a result, we can no longer point to a definite time when a child is no longer considered a child, but is instead an independent young adult. The disengagement of dependency is no longer recognized or celebrated in our culture. This has contributed, in ways that may not be immediately obvious, to a shift in attitudes about child rearing. With the definite boundary between dependent childhood and independent early adulthood effectively gone, there was no longer any recognized point at which children began achieving adultlike independence. Into this vacuum came the voices of the male experts, urging or demanding that all children, both boys and girls, begin realizing the ideal of adulthood—being a separate, independent human being—as early as possible. Since there was no longer an agreed-upon point for childhood to end and adulthood to begin, it became easier to accept the idea that the transition should begin immediately. And it *could* begin immediately, because babies were no longer dependent on their mothers for life-giving breast milk. As a result, the period

The Transition from Dependency to Independence

In most cultures throughout history and throughout the world, children's development—from the total dependence of the infant to the greater independence of the older child—has taken the shape of progress along a gradual continuum, as diagrammed below.

approximate ages

0

1

2

3

4

During the **period of dependency**, babies are carried by their mothers or kept close by them at least most of the time and sleep beside or near their mothers at night. Their need for breast milk limits the amount that they can be separated from their mothers.

5

In the **transition period**, children gradually wean from the breast, from mother's arms, and from the family bed. They gain greater independence from their mothers and take on increasingly complex tasks, whether working or learning.

6

7

8

9

10

11

12

13

14

15

16

17

18

In the **period of developing independence**, children begin to separate from their parents to become young adults. They experience initiation into adulthood (natural for girls, ceremonial for boys). Boys are then taken into the men's world to continue maturing toward manhood; girls remain closer to their mothers as they develop toward womanhood.

allotted for the transition to independence to take place has been compressed so much that, by now, it barely exists.

These developments, although brought about primarily by males and based on the male experience, have given us the methods and approaches most of us now use to raise children of both sexes. The natural boundary that protected the dependency of babies and children on their mothers is gone. Mother herself has become largely dispensable, thanks to the availability of substitutes of every kind. The transition phase from total dependency on the mother to a stage of independence has been reduced to zero. Men—who have taken over as the recognized experts on child rearing—have been given full rein to advocate male gender characteristics, especially the need for independence, and there is no alternative (that is, female-based) point of view that is getting enough attention to check the progress of their argument. We have, in effect, accepted a strange new idea of when to initiate our children into independent separateness that is based neither on natural wisdom nor on scientific analysis of when children are ready to be on their own. The rites now begin at birth.

Further, once the concept of appropriate childhood dependency was abandoned, so too was the idea that children have limited abilities. Instead, the idea took hold that children are not only responsible for nurturing themselves, but are competent to do so.

But nature is wise. Rarely can manipulation and experimentation that is contrary to the basic balance of the universe continue for extended periods. The balance will always reassert itself. I do not mean to suggest that we should, or even can, return to the child-rearing methods of the past. We should not be taken in by the false idea that the ways of other peoples or past generations are necessarily superior to ours. What we need is an approach that is suited to our modern world and our culture, but that also seeks to understand and work with our human natures, rather than trying to deform them, or pretend they don't exist.

I believe we are now seeing the beginnings of that new approach. At the moment, it often takes the form of conflict over whose feelings and opinions about child rearing should be followed—the man's (whether father or doctor or expert) or the woman's. Ironically, this may be happening, in part, because, for several decades now, independence and assertiveness have been encouraged as energetically for girls and women as they have for boys and men. More women therefore have the courage of their convictions, and believe that their opinions and values are valid and important. When such women become mothers, if they find they disagree with their husbands or doctors about how to care for their children, they are more likely to say so and to act on their feelings.

MALE AND FEMALE EXPERTS

Let's take a closer look at the people who provide advice on child rearing today. One of the first things to consider in looking at child-rearing books is the *source* of the information. Who is giving the advice, a man or a woman? With an understanding of the influence of gender on people's approaches to child rearing, we can then put the advice in better perspective. We can begin to make choices based on individual circumstances rather than on the belief that "This is right, and that is wrong," or "This is the way it *should* be done."

Life is complicated, and so is child rearing. There is usually more than one answer to a problem or situation. Yet many of the books, especially those written by men, tell us that if we just follow a certain set of rules or some simple system, we will be virtually guaranteed a glorious child-rearing experience. Many approach this from the opposite direction, implying that if you *fail* to use the suggested system, you are likely to fail as a parent. This plays on parents', especially mothers', fears of not being a good parent. In *You and Your Baby's First Year*, Drs. Sirgay Sanger and John Kelly write, "Like most mothers and fathers, you are probably good at [parenting] already, but we can help you become even better."[3] (Better than whom? I would love to ask.) Another book bears the title *How to Really Love Your Child*, implying that mothers don't really know how to love their children until they read it. In *First Feelings*, Stanley Greenspan, M.D., asks parents, "But how well do you *really* know your baby?"[4] He then goes on to give a detailed analysis aimed at helping parents to begin developing their babies' capacities for self-regulation.

The men who write these books forget—or more likely, never knew—that women's conceptions of what is right for their children may be totally different from theirs. The instructions in some of these books may be scientifically and observationally accurate, from a male point of view. But for many mothers, the instructions are unnecessarily complicated and confusing, and trying to follow them undermines their maternal self-confidence, while at the same time offering no real support for their mothering efforts.

Not all male doctors or writers address mothers in this way. Some have great and useful insights into children's development, maternal emotions, and the need for mother-child bonding. Yet even they tend to write in an assertive, authoritative, characteristically male style that features the must's, do's, and should's for achieving successful bonding and an awareness of your child's developmental stages.

The different perspective women can provide can be seen in an introduction to *Discovering Motherhood*, a book produced by a Virginia-based group of women called Mothers at Home. They say that their book "doesn't tell you how to be a mother—like each of us, you'll find your own way. But the bond uniting mothers is a strong one, and we hope that you'll find this book an affirmation that it is often mothers themselves who can best support and sustain one another."[5] Or consider these introductory words from Dr. Penelope Leach: "Although this is a book, it will not suggest that you do things 'by the book,' but rather that you do them always 'by the baby.'"[6]

Remember, however, that I am talking not so much about male and female individuals, but characteristically male and female approaches. There are a number of women in the child-care field who have adopted a typically male attitude and approach to raising children. Dr. Niles Newton, a behavioral scientist, has said she is very concerned that so many women in our society seem to be becoming, in her word, "masculinized"—that is, taking on male gender characteristics in their approach to child rearing, while suppressing many female ones. There are indeed female doctors, psychologists, and behaviorists who espouse the belief that children should be taught early independence and self-reliance, and whose research reflects a characteristically male perspective on life. These women may be influenced by their (mostly male) teachers, peers, or spouses; they may risk losing approval for their research projects unless they conform to the male approach; or they may have some other reason for feeling that enforcing independence early is a good and loving thing to do.

While there is some advice available from men who support a more nurturing, female-type approach, and from women who support an independent, male-type approach to child rearing, on the whole, the literature does reflect the gender characteristics of the writers. Male

authors tend to stress independence and encourage accomplishments, which they do in direct, authoritative language. Female authors tend to stress connectedness, intimacy, and interdependence, and to do so with a softer
approach and choice of words. Of course, we should remember that the advice of both men and women is given
with good intentions, and is meant to convey what they
believe is best for the child and the family. But understanding that there is usually a difference will allow parents, and especially mothers, to take the best and leave the
rest, with the knowledge that if they disagree—with an
author, or their doctors, or their husbands—they need not
think that they must be wrong. They may just be different.

OUTSTANDING IN THE FIELD?

Historically and globally, advice and help in pregnancy,
childbirth, and child rearing has been handed down from
woman to woman, from mother to daughter, based on
women's own insights, feelings, approaches, and understandings. Yet ironically, despite the rise of women to
positions of great prominence in our society in the past few
decades, and the great emphasis that has been placed on
equal rights for women, the experts people turn to for
advice on child rearing today are still primarily men. In
the United States, the most highly acclaimed books on
child rearing are written by male experts and male researchers. These books usually also receive enthusiastic
endorsements from other well-known men. Every mother
will recognize one if not two or more of the following
names: Benjamin Spock, Lee Salk, T. Berry Brazelton,
James C. Dobson, John Rosemond, Barton Schmitt, Richard Ferber, Alvin Eden, Wayne Dyer, William Sears,
Fitzhugh Dodson, Rudolf Dreikurs, Bruno Bettelheim,
Haim Ginott, Thomas Gordon. There is no lack of books

by women authors, but far fewer have had widespread name recognition, repeated printings, or extended market exposure. Some of the few exceptions are Selma Fraiberg, Louise Bates Ames, and Penelope Leach. A random count of books on library shelves and in bookstores in my area showed that books by women comprised significantly less than half of the books on child care, and a good number of those cover specific topics such as nutrition, breast-feeding, or games for children, rather than providing general child-rearing advice.

The majority of the book endorsements that appear on child-rearing books—those glowing comments on the book jacket that are meant to entice buyers—also come from men, regardless of the gender of the author. If there are endorsements from both a man and a woman, the man's usually appears first. On the dust cover of *Your Child's Health* by Dr. Barton Schmitt we find endorsements from three male doctors, Morris Green (who praises the book as "the most useful and authoritative pediatric guidebook currently available for parents"), T. Berry Brazelton, and Daniel D. Broughton. *You and Your Baby's First Year* by Drs. Sirgay Sanger and John Kelly is endorsed on the front cover by T. Berry Brazelton, M.D., who states, "Excellent. It makes much of the present research available for professionals and parents. Bravo!" A book by Alvin Eden, M.D., *Positive Parenting*, is endorsed by Lendon H. Smith, M.D.

There are some child-care books written by men that have received high acclaim from women. *Nighttime Parenting* by William Sears, M.D., is enthusiastically endorsed by Mary White, a founder of La Leche League International. Dr. Brazelton's *To Listen to a Child* is endorsed by Benjamin Spock, M.D., but also by Louise Bates Ames, Ph.D. *Experts Advise Parents*, written by nine male and five female experts, received an endorsement from Dr. Marianne Neifert, author of *Dr. Mom*, as well as from Dr. Alvin F. Poussaint. But in general, the most commonly available books on child care are written by men and endorsed by men. This only strengthens the general perception that men are the experts on parenting and on advising women how to mother.

MEN INSTRUCT; WOMEN SUGGEST

Men's language is the language of the powerful; it is direct, clear, and succinct, according to Robin Lakoff, author of *Talking Power*.[7] Men easily and comfortably find themselves in positions of dominance and authority. Their child-rearing books tend to instruct the reader; words like *must, do, don't,* and *should* abound. Dr. Barton Schmitt, for example, warns mothers: "*Don't* have the breast become a pacifier." "The child *must* stay in his own bed for the night." [Emphasis added.] Such instructions leave little room for flexibility. Other examples from male writers [all emphasis added]:

- "*Return him* to his bed."

- "*Teach him* to rely on a pacifier or toy.

- "*Avoid conversation* if you feel he should play by himself for awhile."

Even books that express a solid, supportive understanding of mothers and children tend to be quite instructive in style:

- "Parents *must* allow children to feel all their feelings."

- "*Provide* physical outlets.

- "*Use* closeness and touching."

- "*Be ready* to show affection."

- "*Ease tension* through humor."

- *"Help* the child understand the cause of his or her anger."

In his book *How To Raise Happy Kids*, Wayne W. Dyer, M.D., advises parents: *"Laugh* with them. *Concentrate* with [infants] as they grab at a toy or stare intently at an object. *Talk* to them about what they see, praising them when their eyes follow your finger or laugh out loud with them." Men don't waste many words or beat around the bush. They give the facts as they see them and then zero directly in on their advice. As a result, the advice they give frequently comes across as fact rather than opinion. One male author advises his readers that mothers must not become pregnant again until the previous child is at least fifteen months old. I heard about a mother, pregnant for the second time when her first child was eleven months old, who contemplated having an abortion because "the book" had told her she *mustn't* get pregnant so soon. "Men usually have no conception of the power of their words," Lynn Moen, owner of the Birth and Life Bookstore in Seattle, told me.

Not every male-authored book is so obviously direct in style. Two popular child-rearing experts, Drs. T. Berry Brazelton and Lee Salk, frequently take a more expansive approach to a topic before finally homing in on their advice. But when one reads their books in their entirety, the authoritative style, with a more pronounced use of the language of direct instruction, is still noticeable.

Considering men's basic gender characteristics, this style makes sense. Men live in a world of rules and hierarchies, and an authoritative, instructive style of writing—like an authoritative, instructive way of talking—is appropriate for that world. And there is nothing wrong with this approach in and of itself—except that to many women, it can sound *so* authoritative that they react as if it were the truth, instead of being able to see the information as a suggestion or alternative. All advice, whether given by men or by women, is based on opinion, and opinions vary from person to person. But a woman may take the opinion of a male writer as truth even if it isn't true at all, simply because a man's choice of words and style of writing tell her it is. As humorist Jane Campbell says, "Men can speak with such conviction that women may be fooled into thinking they actually know what they're talking about."

Women, who live in a world of cooperative relationships, are more comfortable sharing knowledge than giving instructions. They tend to offer choices or suggestions. "This book increases your parenting options," writes Eileen Shiff in her foreword to *Experts Advise Parents*.[8] Her emphasis is on giving parents choices in child rearing so that they will have a variety of alternatives to try, depending on their own needs and situations. Although what the female experts say may be factual, they tend to write in a style that offers, rather than instructs. Words like *do, must,* and *don't* are used far less frequently. Instead, women writers tend to tread more gently and give detailed explanations rather than short instructions.

In keeping with the female orientation toward human relationships, the emphasis on separation and on teaching self-reliance and independence is usually missing, or at least far less evident, in books written by women. Instead, they focus on what children's needs are and how a parent might go about meeting them. They tend to study the whole child, observing general behavior characteristics and growth patterns, and offer general insights to help readers understand human growth. They frequently acknowledge that there are many gray areas in child rearing. A cartoon I've seen sums up this recognition well. In it, a doctor advises, "All you need to do in child rearing is be consistent." A mother replies, "But how can I be consistent when they never do the same thing twice?"

It was once said that the greatest naturalists do not approach nature as a machine to be taken apart and analyzed piece by piece, or something to control, but that they spend years sitting back and simply looking, observing, and taking notes. The approach of many of the female writers on child rearing tends to follow a similar pattern: They sit back, study, take notes, and then tell us what they have seen—as well as what they have experienced on a daily level with their own children—so that parents can build on their findings and understandings. They tend to give insights and offer suggestions so that parents can match a general understanding with a particular situation.

Compare the difference between male and female advice on the use of playpens. In their respective books, Drs. Alvin Eden and Barton Schmitt both voice the opinion that playpens are quite useful and handy. Dr. Schmitt writes that babies like playpens because they afford a good view of their surroundings. He goes on to say that a baby *should* be introduced to the playpen by four months of age so that he builds up positive associations with it.[9] Dr. Eden states that the playpen "*should* be stocked with interesting, safe objects such as rattles, plastic balls and containers, spoons and lids or pots. . . . Clutch balls and squeaky toys also *should* be provided."[10] [Emphasis added.] The advice is presented as if it were authoritative instruction on the correct way to use a playpen.

Dr. Louise Bates Ames, too, is in favor of using playpens. She says that most babies can spend some time happily playing in a playpen. Instead of explicitly telling parents what to provide, however, she writes, "The ordinarily intelligent and lively mother knows how to embellish the playpen with reasonably interesting toys." There is no suggestion in her writing of authority or dominance. She is not instructing parents, but rather sharing information with other intelligent people, thus giving readers more of a feeling of parental competence. Another female author, Robin Goldstein, writes, *"If you want to encourage your child to spend some time in her playpen, try placing it near you so she can watch you and you can talk or play peek-a-boo with her. . . . You can also try* changing the toys in the playpen frequently so your child will have something different to play with."*[11] [Emphasis added.] The issue here, of course, is not whether playpens are good to use (there are experts, both male and female, who discourage more than occasional use of them), but the different ways the male and female authors approach their discussion of the subject. The men give specific instructions; the women give suggestions and guidelines.

In an area with as many variables as child care, how can we tell who's right? There is an old American Indian story about a lesson taught by the elders to the young men of the tribe. The young braves sit in a circle, in the middle of which is placed a gourd attached to a bit of vine. Each young man is asked to describe what he sees. One describes the shadow as falling on the right side of the vegetable; the person opposite him describes it as falling on the left side. Both differ from the person sitting with his back to the sun, who sees no shadow on the gourd at all. Who describes the gourd correctly? All of them. Their descriptions are merely different.

MEN WATCH THE CLOCK; WOMEN WATCH THE CHILD

Male writers tend to give pragmatic solutions to problems, and many of these involve clocks, schedules, scales, and calendars. They will often instruct parents to take away the breast or the bottle when a child reaches a certain age, to remove their presence from a child for a specified amount of time at a certain age, or to train a child to sleep through the night at a certain age. Generally speaking, they give instructions for training a child toward autonomy—albeit with love—by presenting specific tasks at set times, beginning at a certain age. What that certain age is varies from writer to writer, but most do give one. Women, on the other hand, tend to stress negotiation and watching the development of the child, allowing for the fact that children's needs cannot usually be deduced from the clock or calendar alone because each person brings to a situation his own particular needs, experiences, and readiness. This is in accord with a typical female gender characteristic. To women, each child is an individual, and no calendar can dictate his readiness for any new experience. There is more to readiness than dates on a calendar. As a wise American Indian once said, "With all due respect to the white man's date on the calendar, for us it's just another day."

Asked how a mother should wean her child, Dr. Lee Salk first said, "Gradually." But he then continued, with typical male directness, to say that a mother should show her child how to use a cup when he is between the ages of four and six months. "Do this," he said," while your child is still sucking on the breast or having a bottle." A woman would likely have phrased this as, "At around four to six months, you may want to try offering your baby some juice from a cup." The fact is, though, I was unable to find a book written by a woman from which such a short, quotable section could be taken on this subject, because women's advice on introducing solid foods or drinking from a cup tends to take the form of a discussion rather than a clear-cut instruction.

One male doctor advises using a timer when keeping a child in his chair for time-out disciplinary action, and says that a child should be kept there for one minute for each year of his age, to a maximum of five minutes. He states: "*Carry him* [to his chair or room] facing him away from you. *Don't* lecture or spank on the way. Also, *don't* answer his pleas."[12] [All emphasis added.] A female author, writing on the same topic—the usefulness of time-out—says, "It is better to let the child determine the amount of time she will spend in her room."[13]

On the issue of sleep patterns for babies, several books written by men give detailed schedules. One male doctor gives a table indicating a baby's average hours of sleep. Although he acknowledges that there may be variations of one to two hours in childrens' sleep needs, he nevertheless says that by one week of age a baby should sleep $16\frac{1}{2}$ hours a day; by one month, he should be down to $15\frac{1}{2}$ hours; by three months, 15 hours; by six months, $14\frac{1}{2}$ hours; by nine months, 14 hours; and so on.[14] The idea of timetables and schedules gives many men a feeling of control over their situation, which is something they consider very important. So the concept of schedules just naturally seems to makes sense to them. But from a woman's point of view, schedules can cause a parent to become more focused on the clock than on the child, which breaks the connection between two human beings. And even though some timetables, like the one mentioned above, note that there may be some variation in individual children's requirements, many mothers express concern if their children do not conform to the schedules, because they are presented in such a way, and in such detail, that they seem to represent what a child *should* need. The schedules are not usually offered as information that may—or may not—be useful; they are set up as though they describe the way children should be. Women strive for the approval and liking of others, and motherhood touches the very core of their concern. If her baby has difficulty fitting into the schedule, a mother may fear that she is somehow incompetent. Thus, what is meant to be a guideline becomes an indicator of her competence as a mother. Further, she may unconsciously fear that if she proves incompetent, she may lose the love and approval of her peers, her friends, or her family. She is then faced with the impossible situation of wanting to conform so that she will be thought of as a good mother, but having no means to achieve this because her baby has his own needs, his own "schedule."

In addition to devising precise schedules, men are usually much more at ease in instructing people that they absolutely must follow them. Women, on the other hand, feel more compelled to "talk things out" and come to a consensus. "Since women are particularly concerned with the feelings of others," writes Cris Evatt, "they are uncomfortable with direct orders that can wound the ego of the other person."[15] A mother named Mary Ellen told me that she always tried to gain her daughter's cooperation by talking with her. Her husband, on the other hand, not being so concerned about a possible break in connectedness with his child, found it much easier to use authoritative discipline. He was quicker to place the child on a chair or send her to her room for ten minutes. When their daughter became older, Mary Ellen said, this method was indeed effective. However, when she was asked if she would use it on a young child, she replied, "Oh, no. I just don't feel the need to be so strict with a little child." To her, communication and interaction made more sense than going strictly by rules or the clock.

"Men would rather try to solve problems than worry about them," writes Evatt. "They want action. Men tend to be more pragmatic, matter-of-fact and less emotional about issues."[16] Men tend to approach the study of child rearing by analyzing problems and then giving detailed instructions on how to solve them. One doctor assures parents that a baby's waking at night is not bad behavior, but that the child does need to learn the habit of falling asleep by himself. He instructs the reader to let the baby cry for five minutes the first night, then for longer and longer periods on subsequent nights, until the child gives up and no longer cries for his parents. He suggests using a timer because, as he acknowledges, listening to a baby screaming without doing something may be difficult for parents.[17]

A videotape of this method being used by an actual family was shown on national television. Viewers saw a young child arching his back and screaming uncontrollably as he faced the horror of abandonment in his crib. The method did eventually achieve what it was meant to; after three nights, the baby succumbed, gave up, and lay down. I couldn't help but wonder, however, why doing such a thing and ignoring a little baby's terrified sobbing wasn't considered a form of child abuse. I also have doubts that this method has been well thought out as a means of inducing children to change their behavior. In some cultures, a loudly crying child (or even an older baby) may be isolated to teach him correct behavior—not to make so much noise—but when he stops, he is rewarded by immediate reentry into the community. With a method like the doctor's, above, however, when a child has been isolated in his bed at night and cries until he finally gives up, what is his reward? Nothing! Only more loneliness. There is no positive reinforcement for the desired behavior. The child is left alone, as if forgotten.

Not that we should assume that this doctor is malicious. He is giving advice that he genuinely feels is best for the baby and the family. Although he has recently softened his stance somewhat, he believes that it is vitally important that children learn to be independent and sleep by themselves. And again, it is not only men who accept this characteristically male perspective on the importance of independence. Many women today, like their counterparts of a century ago, may welcome this advice because they themselves are under so much stress. With so many mothers working full-time jobs as well as a second shift at home, trying to meet the often conflicting demands of employer, husband, children, and household, and dealing with feelings of guilt that they aren't able to spend more time with their children, it is no wonder that such methods have widespread support. After awhile, stress makes people focus on protecting their own sanity. Almost anyone, when under enough stress, will eventually say in desperation, "But what about me? I need my space, too. I need some time to myself. I need some rest."

MEN STRESS CONTROL; WOMEN STRESS CHOICES

"You may decrease nighttime nursing sessions by one minute each night or two and increase the minimum times between nursing in the same manner," writes a male doctor and syndicated newspaper columnist.[18] To him, this is logical advice that will give a mother control over her child and the weaning process. This is based on the frequent male assumption that a child who breast-feeds on demand is actually controlling his mother. To a person living in a hierarchical world (as men generally do) this means that the child has "won" and the mother has "lost." The natural response to this is to "fight back," to reassert control. After all, he reasons, if you don't, the little tyke could decide to call the shots and nurse forever. "Don't let them wrap you around their little finger!" they warn. Having the mother "in control" of the weaning process puts the adult back in the dominant position, which is what feels right to many men.

This line of reasoning is entirely lost on most breast-feeding mothers (and babies). To look at it as a matter of who is controlling whom is foreign to them. A woman is likely to say that it is ludicrous to talk about controlling an emotional or physical need. It would be like telling a young husband to reduce the amount of time he spends having loving thoughts about his wife by one minute each day. Mothers tend to feel little need to control, because their primary interest lies in bonding and connecting. To them, this is what makes the world feel safe, and right. If anything, schedules threaten their ability to keep an intimate connection with the baby alive, something they feel an innate need to do. In short, while men try to prevent themselves from being pushed *around*, women try to prevent themselves from being pushed (or pushing someone else) *away*.

One mother told the story of her husband, who was adamant about their baby getting used to taking a bath. He insisted on this daily routine even though the infant protested loudly. He argued that eventually the baby would get used to it. He wanted control over bathtime, and was not going to let the child decide whether a bath was necessary or not. The mother couldn't see why he was making a major issue out of forcing baths rather than looking to see if there were any alternatives. She called a friend in desperation. "There must be more than one way to clean a baby!" she cried over the phone.

Many man feel that we must actively control our children because if we don't, we will "lose control" of them, and then we will have a "problem" on our hands—children who will not stay in their beds all night, or who will not clean their plates, or who will not stay with a babysitter. A problem, by definition, is something that shouldn't be or shouldn't happen. But I submit that many of these so-called problems are not so much a sign that something is wrong with the child, but that adults are unwilling to allow children to be children, with childlike needs, wants, and capabilities.

Because they feel no need to be in control or dominate, women are more likely to allow for a variety of approaches rather than feeling they must choose and advocate only one. In *Women and Mothers*, Sheila Kitzinger writes: "I have learned that telling people how they ought to behave creates more problems than it solves, and all too often means that they are unable to adapt to challenges confronting them, because instead of flexibility they are armed with a series of magic formulae which they hope will work when the going gets difficult. It is much more valuable to give people information and self-confidence so that they can make their own informed choices in terms of the reality they face."[19] Or as Eda LeShan, columnist and author of *When Your Child Drives You Crazy*, says: "We are lucky to have so many people spending so much time studying childhood. But we need to understand that no matter how much we learn, there will never be simple panaceas for anything as important, complex, exciting and mysterious as raising children."[20]

MEN STRESS INDEPENDENCE; WOMEN STRESS INTERDEPENDENCE

"But how do you teach a child independence when he sleeps in your family bed?" Whether it is a question concerning the family bed, breast-feeding on demand, picking a baby up when he cries, or not leaving a child with a babysitter before he is ready for the separation, the question is asked time and again by parents, especially fathers: "But what about teaching them independence?"

Dr. T. Berry Brazelton, one of the most popular experts on child rearing in this country, says that our society values and demands independence. Life in our present-day Western culture, he maintains, is much more difficult than it is in cultures where children are not forced into early independence. Our society demands an unusually high number of task-oriented accomplishments of children, such as competing with aggressive peers in play groups, attending nursery school, and sitting still in kindergarten.[21] Because of the stresses of daily life, Dr. Brazelton and other experts say, discipline to enforce independence and self-comforting is a must.

Admittedly, our world of computers, high-speed travel, violent television shows, parents who both work all day, daycare centers, and babysitters creates stressful situations. But are things here really any more stressful than they are in other parts of the world, where people experience famines, droughts, wars, disease, violence, oppression, poverty, and overcrowding? In fact, most of us live in a world of relative calm and abundance of every kind: food, medicine, housing, comparative safety, and a nation at peace. Furthermore, no matter where a child finds himself—in a peaceful hamlet, a war-torn city, a famine-stricken country, or a household full of go-getters in a high-speed modern metropolis—his basic need for unconditional love, security, bonding, and connectedness is the same. And does it really make sense to prepare children for a stressful world by *creating* stress in them from infancy on?

Dr. Brazelton says that, after thirty years of practice in pediatrics, he has become convinced that, "while independence may not be an easy goal for parents to accept, it is an exciting and rewarding goal for the child. . . . It will develop positive self image and give him a feeling of strength."[22] He feels that children's lack-of-independence problems are caused by their inability to comfort themselves with what he calls a "lovey," a toy or blanket to which the child can turn at any time. So many problems could be solved, he says, if children were just taught "self comforting." A child could then soothe himself when hurt or frightened or having difficulty falling asleep; his mother's presence would not be necessary. Dr. Brazelton feels that the "lovey" stage is a necessary step toward learning independence and self-reliance. Dr. Benjamin Spock also takes this view, saying that when a child is able to receive comfort from a material rather than a maternal comforter, he can be soothed yet still retain his independence from his mother.[23]

For years I agonized over how it was possible that gentle, learned, thoughtful men could so easily find a "lovey," a mere material thing, a reasonable substitute for a mother's loving arms. There is an enormous amount of evidence that children have a deep emotional need to connect with their mother or another human being, not an object. Some of this evidence comes from the work of male researchers, some from women themselves. Yet the idea that it is better for children to depend on a pacifier or a doll still prevails. Why? Because men like Drs. Brazelton and Spock, two of the most highly respected men in their field, continue to promote it.

As we have seen, from a man's point of view, independence is exciting. To be independent poses challenges and offers rewards; it gives a feeling of mastery and allows one to negotiate status in a hierarchical world; it encourages emotional and mental stretching, exploration, and curiosity. Interdependence and intimacy, on the other hand, are often confused with dependency, which men tend to equate with weakness. A mother may agonize over the apparent insensitivity when she hears, "Let the child cry. He has to learn to become independent." Yet her male doctor or counterpart is merely speaking out of his own felt need, and his wish for the child to achieve the fulfillment of that need.

It is not that the male writers who promote the use of the "lovey" do not recognize children's need for intimacy and connectedness, at least on some level. In fact, the whole concept of the "lovey" is proof that they do recognize it. But they are looking at children through the filter of their own gender characteristics, projecting their own need for independence onto children and calling it a "need in society." They simply cannot give up the belief that being independent of mother is of paramount importance in a child's life, no matter what his age. Since they know that a young child needs a source of comfort on which he can depend—but the idea that it might be appropriate for a child's mother to be that comforter has been rejected—the "lovey" has been invented.

In a way, these men may have a point about independence being a "need in society"—if you consider that our society's values are based largely on male rather than female or maternal ones. But the question of why this is so, or of whether we should be content to let it remain so, is never addressed. As Dr. Deborah Tannen writes, it is an accepted tenet of contemporary American psychology that mental health requires early psychological separation from one's parents.[24] And who is it that dictates contemporary American psychology? There is no shortage of women in the field, but men are generally considered the leading experts, just as they are in the field of child rearing.

In my experience, women writers tend to cover the topic of independence only because they know our society has made such an issue of it. Breast-nurturing women who allow baby-led weaning know from experience that independence occurs naturally, or with a little encouragement, when the time is right. To them, it's like sleeping; when you've slept enough, you wake up and want to get up. If they were to find themselves in a society that was very concerned about the ability to wake up after a certain number of hours of sleep, they would probably feel the need to say that waking up is indeed important—but would add that there's no need to worry about it; it will happen in due time.

Do we really have to train our children to become independent? Differences of opinion about this have caused feelings of guilt and anger in this mother, when blame was placed on her for not "training" her child to go to the dentist by herself. It has caused pain for many mothers who have tried to "train" their children to sleep by themselves and had to listen to sobbing for hours on end. It has also caused anger and frustration in some fathers, who have seen their wives not establishing clear-cut rules and forcing their children to stand on their own two feet.

Irene Josselyn, M.D., past member of the Southern California Psychoanalytic Institute, made an astute observation on the concept of training. We "train" a dog, she wrote in *Psychological Development of Children* in 1967, "because we wish him to behave and become different in our home than his inherent nature would dictate. So we train him to be and act according to our wishes and convenience. We have taken the dog away from his natural environment and out of necessity train him to fit into ours. Civilization did not rise within the prehistoric society because of *training* but because . . . human beings *need* others of [their] own species."[25] Likewise, children grow and become independent not because we train them to, but because it is their inherent nature to do so. Children, in their natural environment, need love, support, and encouragement to develop their "undeniable quest for independence, autonomy, the indefatigable will to grow, learn, master biological, social, psychological and intellectual endeavors," as Diana Bert et al. write in *After Having a Baby*.[26]

In fact, mothers do encourage their children to become independent, by nursing or comforting or soothing them *only* when they ask for their maternal or another human comforter. "Don't offer, but don't refuse, either," say some mothers. Children will ask for only as much nurturing as they need. The child who has no anxiety about being abandoned or losing connectedness, intimacy, and the security of being loved by another human being usually develops a superb feeling of security in himself, a feeling that in turn allows him to be truly independent, or interdependent, according to his needs. "A child whose needs are met and who has a strong attachment to his parents will develop a foundation of trust that will allow him to become independent," writes Robin Goldstein in *Everyday Parenting.*[27]

This is also a wonderful way to foster the development of self-esteem at the time when it should develop, in childhood. "High self-esteem" and "low self-esteem" have become catch phrases among therapy groups that claim to help adults find the "hurt child" within themselves, with the promise that they will be able to heal, or at least come to grips with, the hurts and stresses of childhood. For people who are hurting, it's better to find comfort late than never. But perhaps the popularity of this type of therapy for adults is also telling us that we should nurture and support our biological children, not just our "inner" children. If we do, perhaps they won't need remedial classes in self-esteem when they grow up.

When reading books on the subject of child rearing, a red flag should go up in our minds if the advice presented just doesn't make sense to us. We must always remember the author's point of departure, and gender makeup is a critical part of this. Mothers especially should learn to see the gender traits behind the advice, to see beyond the authoritative style of so many male writers, and to remember that their own feelings and observations are valid and important. And men should understand that theirs is not the only point of view that makes any sense. After all, they would be unlikely to accept "expert" advice from a woman on something uniquely male that they do every day. When we turn to the books for guidance in a particular situation, we should all ask ourselves what it is that they are really saying, why they're saying it, and above all, what is best for our children.

Chapter 5

The Importance of the Nurturing Mother

Mothers and babies have had extended, intimate relationships since the days of our first primate ancestors, over 65 million years ago. This characteristically human behavior is a natural result of the symbiosis between babies' innate needs and mothers' innate gender characteristics. Only relatively recently, a mere 100 or so years ago, did we come to think that the human species is so infinitely modifiable that we can deny or ignore this basic, natural part of life. As a result, the mother-child relationship has been more altered during this last century in our Western society than ever before in human history. At no other time have babies and young children been subject to as much experimentation and as many variations in handling as they are today.

Nor have parents ever been subjected to so much conflicting advice. Rock your child. Don't rock your child. Breast-feed your baby. Bottle-feed your baby. Answer every cry. Let the child cry it out alone. Be permissive. Be strict. Use spankings to discipline. Never spank your child. Feed only according to a strict schedule. Allow a child to eat when hungry. Start teaching reading at age two. Don't teach reading until the child is ready. Leave your baby with babysitters from birth on. Don't leave your baby with a babysitter until she is ready. Daycare centers are okay. Daycare centers are alarmingly dangerous. Teach independence at an early age. Allow a child to become independent gradually. Hold your child when she wants to be held. Teach your child to hug a "lovey" instead.

In part, we have all of these decisions to make because we face an unprecedented array of options in child care. Until approximately the turn of the century, a baby's natural need for milk dictated that she be nursed by her mother, or in some cases a wet nurse, which necessitated at least a certain amount of responsiveness and holding. Prior to that time, if a child was separated from this early intimacy, it was likely to be a result of parental death, whether caused by disease, famine, or war. Such children might be cared for by other relatives or placed in institutions; in extreme cases they died, from disease or lack of sufficient human contact. The major change in an assured period of intimacy for most children began when bottle-feeding became the preferred method of feeding babies. Since then, such developments as playpens, pacifiers, separate sleeping rooms, and daycare centers have contributed to the trend toward separating young babies from close contact with their primary caretakers.

TRADITIONAL CHILD-REARING PRACTICES

Infant- and child-rearing practices vary all over the world. In some cultures, babies are carried in their mothers' arms, while in others they are tightly swaddled and placed on cradleboards. Among some groups, babies sleep in their parents' beds, while in others they sleep in a cradle next to the mother's side of the bed. In some cultures, bowel and bladder control are trained; in others, the child is merely guided when she seems ready. In some societies, a child touches human skin almost continuously. In others, she is wrapped in much clothing.

In warmer climates, babies tend to be carried more and longer, and closer to the body of the caretaker, than in colder climates, where cradles, carriers, and cradleboards are more commonly used for at least part of the day (although always under the watchful eyes of a caretaker).[1] In Africa, for instance, babies spend most of their waking hours being carried on someone's back or in-arms. (Through magazines like *National Geographic*, most of us have seen photographs of this common practice.) At night, they sleep next to their mothers on a mat or platform, with prolonged skin-to-skin contact.

In the Northern Hemisphere, the use of the cradleboard was (and in some places still is) more common. A cradleboard can be carried on a person's back, suspended from rafters or a tree branch, where it can sway back and forth, or hung on the side of a horse. Many people can recall seeing a photographic image of a Native American mother with a cradleboard either on her lap or leaning against a tree close to where she is working. Anthropologist John M. Whiting postulates that the use of the cradleboard may stem from the fact that an infant's sleeping hours do not correspond with those of adults, and separate cradling may provide a more effective way of maintaining proper body temperature.[2] Not all societies in colder climates use cradleboards, however. An Inuit mother in the Canadian Arctic will carry her child on her back in a specially designed pouch that is part of her fur parka or *amantik*. Children are carried in this fashion until they are two or three years old.[3]

The duration of the breast-nurturing period is extremely variable, ranging from one to nine years, with an average of one to two years. Whether or not a child is permitted to nurse until she wishes to stop is for the most part determined by the society she lives in. Since different societies have different attitudes, we range from the extreme of no breast-feeding at all (or a minimal few days or weeks) in the United States to eight or nine years elsewhere in the world. In *Mothering Your Nursing Toddler*, Norma Jane Bumgarner gives numerous examples of peoples around the world who routinely nurse well past what would be an accepted age in the United States. Ancient Egyptian custom allowed children to nurse until they were well past their third year. Primitive subcultures such as the Arapesh or the Siriano in Bolivia, or the Zinacanteco Indians in Mexico, allow breast-feeding for extended periods. In China, children up to five years old have been recorded nursing, especially if the mother has not had another baby in the meantime. Perhaps the longest recorded nursing time comes from India, where it is believed that the longer a child nurses, the longer she will live. Mothers therefore nurse for as long as their children want to, which in some cases can mean up to eight or nine years. (When a child nurses for such a long time, she is no longer nursing for nutritional reasons. If a mother does not have another baby in the meantime, which would stimulate the milk flow, her breasts will stop producing milk when her child is around five or six years old.) In the United States, there are some mothers who allow their children to nurse for as long as they want, anywhere from two to seven years. It takes a totally confident, self-accepting attitude and a relaxed discreetness, however, to do so in our society, where until recently, nursing for six months was considered long. One American mother I know asked her six-year-old daughter why she was still nursing. The child smiled and said in a surprised voice, "Because I like it," as if to say, "Isn't that obvious?"

How long a child nurses, or where she sleeps or spends her waking hours, may not be nearly as important, however, as how she is treated as an integral part of the family, how her cries are answered, and whether she is assured sufficient intimate contact with her mother or mother substitute, or is left alone to mother or feed herself.

THE IMPORTANCE OF BONDING

According to a Hindu doctrine, what we want out of life is love fulfillment, the knowledge that there is a future, and the ability to play with curiosity. This starts at birth, with the love fulfillment of mother-infant bonding. The desire for intimacy and connectedness is inherent in most women, so mothers enjoy the intimacy, too. Even the most hurried and stressed-out mothers usually strive for connectedness with their children.

The feeling of intimacy and closeness that develops between a mother and her child is often compared to the experience of falling in love in adult life. When this early love is free of frustration, anger, disappointment, and fear of abandonment, a child stands a much better chance of finding secure love as an adult, according to child development specialist Selma Fraiberg.[4] A child whose cries have been answered and whose emotional needs have been met, and who has not been taxed by having to handle feelings of hurt, pain, or fright when she is too young, grows up with a high level of self-esteem. She has been shown that she is worth listening to and being taken seriously. She grows up feeling worthwhile, and is unlikely to become an anguished adult forever trying to "find herself" or defeat an inferiority complex.

Twentieth-century Western culture, however, practices extraordinary routine separation. From birth on, most babies are separated from their mothers a great deal of the time. It has been estimated that shortly after giving birth, the average Western mother is in close contact with her infant only 25 percent of the time; this drops to approximately 5 percent after a few weeks.[5] Babies are placed in cribs to sleep, suckled on bottles and pacifiers, and placed in strollers, playpens, and walkers. The sounds of a crying baby (which many experts encourage parents to ignore at least some of the time) are drowned out by television and radio. Many infants, Fraiberg writes, are dropped off at daycare centers to spend the day with other crying children. Their mothers must rush off to work, "unable, like her ancient Greek, Mexican, Chinese and Indian sisters, to work with her child by her side," as Susan B. Tobey says in *Art of Motherhood.*[6]

Never before has such adult behavior been expected of such young children. They are required to handle, without protest, all kinds of stressful situations, particularly separation from intimacy with loved ones. Great efforts are directed toward making children hurry to grow up, either because it is felt to be good for them or because it lessens their demands on adults, who are dealing with personal and professional stresses of their own.

It is ironic that it isn't until something becomes seriously endangered that we begin to gather information, knowledge, and wisdom about it, whether the subject is the family or the rain forests. "The more we learn about the conditions that undergird and foster the development of human competence and character, the more we see these same conditions being eroded and destroyed in contemporary societies," writes Uri Bronfenbrenner, professor of psychology as well as of human development and family studies at Cornell University.[7] Just as breast-feeding seemed on the verge of extinction in our part of the world during the 1950s and 1960s, great amounts of research data became available that showed its distinct advantages and benefits. The more popular it became to separate mothers and children, placing increasing stress on the children, the more studies began to warn of the negative consequences of early enforced separation.

"I suggest," writes Australian psychoanalyst Dr. Peter Cook, "that childrearing in English speaking societies is emerging from an era in which many widely held beliefs, values, attitudes and practices have been so out of harmony with the genetically influenced nature and needs of mothers and their developing children, that they have contributed to conflict, stress and emotional and behavioral disturbances in the infant and developing child."[8] The result of our modern Western style of child rearing, Dr. Cook feels, has been a basic distrust of children. We are inclined to see children as selfish and demanding, rather than as naturally immature and dependent on parents to meet their needs. We try to mold our children according to predetermined patterns, rather than seeking to give them what they need and to develop a cooperative, mutually satisfying, affectionate relationship.[9]

We aren't suspicious only of children; by extension, we tend to distrust maternal emotions as well. When a child wants to be held and cuddled, and her mother wants to respond to her needs and hold her, many of the reigning child-rearing experts, who want to stress independence, come forth with explanations of why the mother's interpretation of her child's needs is wrong. We are told that the baby only wants to manipulate her, and that her response and desire for intimacy are therefore inappropriate. If a mother follows this "expert" advice, the end result is that her child's needs are not met, her own needs go unfulfilled, and a strain is put on the development of a trusting, loving relationship between the two.

A child who has been forced to accept, after nights of terrified screaming, that her parents will not come to her rescue, will seem to give up and accept her condition. One cannot but wonder, however, what lasting effect this feeling of abandonment, this rage, this fear will have on her for the rest of her life. It is a powerful experience to call for another human being and be ignored. Throughout the ages, shunning has been used as one of the worst punishments in many societies. Whether among Australian aborigines, ancient Roman citizens, Amish farmers, or West Point cadets, "the worst sanction the community can issue is shunning. The person ignored grows gradually depressed, and soon begins to doubt his or her very existence," according to Mihaly Csikszentmihalyi, Ph.D., former chairman of the psychology department at the University of Chicago. The world becomes a very large, empty, hostile place. Many people feel a sense of emptiness when they are alone. Adults overwhelmingly report that their worst experiences have taken place when they were alone, Dr. Csikszentmihalyi notes.[10]

According to Dr. Csikszentmihalyi, "We are biologically programmed to find other human beings the most important objects in the world."[11] For young children, other human beings are not only the most important objects, but virtually the only important objects. A child needs to have her cries answered so that she learns the meaning and rewards of communication. It might seem outrageous to compare the practice of shunning with the relatively short lessons in aloneness we give our children, such as learning to fall asleep or handle fear and pain alone. But how do we know how much aloneness is too much, how long is too long, or at what age a child can handle it? Adults can talk about their experiences. Young children cannot. For a young child, the future is now. When there has been a letdown in love fulfillment and a child experiences physical or emotional pain, there is a break in feeling good about life, good about love, good about oneself.

I know of parents who are spending an exorbitant

amount of money on a psychiatrist for their little girl because the child refuses to sleep by herself or stay with a babysitter. The irony of this is that the child may be the healthiest one of them all; she knows there is something wrong with having to handle aloneness before she is ready, and she is doing all she can to try to convey this to her parents. "Pity the child," wrote Deborah Jackson in *Three in a Bed*, "who has withdrawn into a resigned silence."[12] But her parents have become convinced that there is something terribly wrong with their child, that she is being too stubborn and self-centered. (Actually, her mother confided to me that she had not seen anything really wrong with her little girl, but "everybody else" kept telling her the child had "problems of over-attachment.")

Much emphasis has been placed on making sure that a child grasps the meaning of independence, supposedly to ensure that she becomes an emotionally well-balanced person. Yet sales of self-help books and books on how to increase one's self-esteem are at record levels and still growing. According to *Newsweek*, an estimated 15 million Americans attend support groups regularly.[13] This phenomenon cannot be attributed solely to a premature push for childhood independence, of course. But it is certainly clear that all of the stress on independence has failed to prevent people from developing unhealthy dependencies. It seems, in fact, reasonable to wonder if it has not actually contributed to the feelings of emptiness and co-dependencies, real or imagined, from which many people suffer today.

John Bowlby, M.D., a psychiatrist, psychoanalyst, and mental health consultant to the World Health Organization, wrote in *Child Care and the Growth of Love*, "Among the most significant developments of psychiatry . . . has been the steady growth of evidence that the quality of the parental care which a child receives in his earliest years is of vital importance for his future mental health. Deprivation research demonstrates the serious impact on infants and young children of the absence of a mother, even though basic physical needs are met; and this raises a question of how it is that a mother promotes the normal development of a child. The answer obviously lies in the interaction that she has with him."[14]

Herbert Ratner, M.D., member of the La Leche League Medical Advisory Board and editor of *Child and Family*, has commented, "Leading authorities agree that for optimum development the child needs one person as a full-time caretaker for the first three years, a person who has time day and night to devote herself to the needs of the child."[15] And Harold M. Voth, M.D., senior psychiatrist with the Menninger Foundation, has said, "A baby must have a mother, a mother who is mature enough to attend to its needs and provide so-called object constancy for a minimum of three years. *The mothering function is one of the most important of all human events but, unfortunately, one of the least appreciated or regarded by society.*"[16] [Emphasis added.]

WHAT CHILDREN NEED

A child needs to establish a trusting, bonded relationship with another person, as a precursor to all of the relationships she will experience for the rest of her life. A child needs to be assured safety from outside dangers. And a child needs to be touched. "The manner in which the young of all mammals snuggle and cuddle against the body of the mother and against the bodies of their siblings or of any other introduced animal strongly suggests that cutaneous stimulation is an important biological need, for both their physical and their behavioral development," writes Ashley Montagu, Ph.D., in *Touching: The Human Significance of the Skin.*[17]

One of the reasons for this is that an infant at birth is not completely developed. The rate of growth of the human brain during the last few months in the womb is so great that vaginal birth would be impossible if gestation lasted longer than approximately nine months.[18] Some scientists maintain that it takes another nine months after birth before the baby is ready for less than total dependence on her mother; some say it takes longer. During this period, the child needs a great deal of continuous, intimate interaction with her mother as she gradually becomes ready for an independent life. A recognition of the urgent need for closeness is evident in the numerous "loveys"—blankets, teddy bears, and dolls—that babies and young children are surrounded with, especially when they spend time alone. What is not always recognized, however, is that what a baby really needs is intimacy with another human being, not an inanimate object.

Babies need motion to experience a release of tension. Since a baby cannot move very much by herself, her energies and tension must be released through the motion others provide for her. Most parents (and many non-parents) know that picking up a crying or fussy baby and walking with her, bouncing her, or taking her for a ride will help her quiet down. Many people, especially mothers, unconsciously sway gently from side to side when they hold a baby, or gently bounce or roll a baby carriage back and forth. This is done even when the baby is perfectly content.

Motion is very relaxing. It helps to bring a baby back into equilibrium when she is tense. Some people even feel that carrying a baby while walking or working in the home or yard causes a symbiotic transfer and release of energy between both adult and child. In any case, parents who carry their babies on their persons much of the day usually have very contented children. Both of my own children spent a great deal of their first few years either in-arms or in a back carrier, and they were quite content there as long as I was busy. Babies want and need motion, and plenty of it, especially the kind of motion that comes from contact with another person, rather than from an automatic swing or some other mechanical device.

For the first five to seven months of life, a baby needs superb nutrition but her digestive system is too immature to tolerate and assimilate the benefits of most foods. Experts agree that breast milk is unequaled as a source of nourishment for young babies. It also helps boost a baby's immunity to diseases, because in addition to nutrients it contains antibodies manufactured by her mother's immune system that the baby's own, immature immune system could not produce.[19]

The nutritional composition of breast milk is initially a slightly modified version of the nutrition a baby receives from her mother in utero. After birth, both the quality and quantity of breast milk change, as the baby herself grows and changes, so that it is always perfect for her body's needs. As time goes by and she needs it less and less, the supply of milk diminishes and finally ceases altogether.[20]

In addition to the nutritional and immune-system benefits, breast-feeding gives a child the advantage of much touching and closeness with her mother, and it activates all of her senses; in addition to the obvious taste and smell associated with feeding, a nursing infant sees her mother, hears her voice and her heartbeat, feels her touch and experiences movement through frequent changes in position. Selma Fraiberg writes, "If we read the biological program correctly, the period of breastfeeding [for one to two years] insures continuity of mothering as part of the program for the formation of human bonds."[21]

Another benefit of that female specialty, breast-feeding, is that it helps with child spacing. Mothers who nurse their babies are less likely to become pregnant than those who don't. This allows a woman's body to recuperate naturally from pregnancy and childbirth, while assuring that her baby will have an optimum length of time for bonding and intimacy with her. There had been some speculation that the act of breast-feeding itself inhibits ovulation. But further research has shown that feeding from the breast alone is not enough; continuous closeness between mother and child appears to be more important. When a mother remains close to her child, both during the day and at night, it can lengthen amenorrhea, the absence of menstruation.[22] For most women to stay amenorrheic, they and their babies must remain virtually inseparable. This may sound like an impossible assignment to us today. But women who try it, and who are supported in doing so by family and friends, often find that it is not impossible or disturbing at all. They carry their babies on their persons and proceed with their work, or work with the child close by, and their babies sleep in their beds with them at night.

Constant contact between mother and child—especially having a young child sleep with her mother—may also play a role in the prevention of Sudden Infant Death Syndrome (SIDS). The cause of SIDS remains unknown, according to the National Institutes of Child Health and Human Development, despite extensive, thorough case investigations, complete autopsies, examinations of death scenes, and reviews of clinical histories. But SIDS researcher Dr. James McKenna writes that "from a purely scientific point of view—given the special biological vulnerabilities of human infants, who are born with only 25 percent of their adult brain capacity—there may well be a subclass of the overall heterogenous SIDS population for which the parental sensory cues (touch, movement, breathing sounds, smells, temperature exchange, and partner-induced arousals) and the parental monitoring provided in a co-sleeping microenvironment inhibit the expression of some SIDS deficits."[23]

Dr. McKenna notes, "Co-family sleeping in humans, during at least the first year, is a universal, specieswide normative context for infant sleep, to which both parents and infants are biologically and psychosocially adapted."[24] Having infants sleep separately from their mothers is a very recent, and arguably an unnatural, experience for them. Could it be, he asks, that this may be a cause of—or at least contribute to causing—SIDS? The pattern of infants sleeping close to or beside their mothers "has developed over at least 4 million years of evolution as a specific response to the biological and social needs of the human infant," he writes, to which I would add that it is probably a response to the biological and social needs of the mother as well.[25]

In many cultures, constant closeness between mothers and babies is the norm. In many of these same cultures, a woman who conceives before her previous child has achieved a certain level of development—is walking, for instance—is considered shamed.[26] But in Western culture in the 1900s, natural child spacing ceased to occur, as mothers were increasingly separated from their babies. Children were often born in rapid succession, sometimes no more than twelve or eighteen months apart. Overwhelmed by caring alone for more children than ever before, women may have been more willing to accept the idea that early independence is best; the more children could do for themselves, the less overworked their mothers would be. One development led to and reinforced the other, and we moved further and further away from closeness and intimacy between mothers and babies.

The implications of close bonding between mother and child are many. Perhaps one day we will know them all. But this much we do know: All babies thrive on being held, cuddled, carried, and breast-nurtured; breast milk is the ideal food for the growing infant; children suffer, emotionally and psychologically, when they have to endure forced separation; and children who are given unconditional love as babies and who are allowed to wean away from their mothers at an unhurried pace are more likely to grow up to be well-adjusted, independent adults.

WOMEN AS MOTHERS

An Arabic saying tells us, "God could not be everywhere; therefore he made mothers." The poet William Makepeace Thackeray wrote, "Mother is the name for God on the lips and hearts of little children." If we were to design a mother, what kind of person would we create? Is there any reason that nature has made women the primary caretakers and nurturers of young children?

One must always exercise caution in asking the question, "What did nature intend?" because we can see nature only through the filter of our own experiences and preconceived ideas. Human concepts and interpretations of what is "natural" come in innumerable variations. Moreover, we would not always *want* to be subject to what nature "intends," if it threatens our health or safety. But we are part of nature nevertheless, and it behooves us to look at the implications of that fact and respect them.

How has nature ensured the continuation of life? By endowing us with emotions and feelings that make procreation and caring for offspring inherently pleasurable and desirable. And the nurturing that is a natural expression of women's basic gender characteristics—especially the drive to connect and form close bonds with others—is just what babies and young children thrive on. Not all women make for wonderful mothers, of course. Nor are men lacking in the ability to love and nurture children. But

generally, generically, there is every indication that nature
has made a favorable match between women and babies.
They complement each other best, most of the time.

There are an increasing number of studies that "prove"
nature has set up intriguing ways to assure that a connectedness and intimacy between mother and child occurs.
Studies by Marshall H. Klaus, M.D., and John H. Kennel,
M.D., show that mothers who have close, preferably skin-
to-skin, contact with their babies immediately following
birth are more likely to breast-feed their children.[27] Such
physical contact may also create a significant long-term
difference in mothering behavior, especially notable in
those women who do go on to breast-feed, as compared to
mothers who are separated from their babies at birth or
who bottle-feed their babies.[28]

Breast-feeding releases a hormone, prolactin, that
stimulates a woman's desire to nurse and be intimate with
her child. This is especially helpful for first-time mothers,
who may be troubled by feelings of inadequacy or lack of
knowledge about infant care. This hormonal response
helps a woman enjoy the intimacy of her relationship with
her child. Not infrequently, a woman who is pregnant for
the first time expresses the concern that she will be bored
being at home with a baby, and is afraid that she will feel
"stuck," alone, with nothing to do. But once the baby
arrives, she is often surprised to feel a tremendous joy in
her intimacy and connectedness with her child. In breast-
feeding mothers, especially, this feeling can last for several
years. Breast-nurturing gives many mothers a totally ful-
filled feeling. They feel whole when they are close to their
babies and answer their cries. While it gives them pride
and joy to see their children manifest accomplishments on
their own, they always know that, no matter how self-sufficient their children become, there will always be a special
bond between them.

This is not to say that bottle-feeding mothers lack strong feelings of connectedness with their infants; nature has made sure that they do, for the sake of the children. But bottle-feeding mothers tend to look upon feeding more as something that is done because of a physical necessity and a desire to soothe a hungry baby, to do something for and with the child. Most breast-feeding mothers, on the other hand, find the very act of breast-feeding to be something that is physically pleasurable for themselves, as well as emotionally fulfilling.[29] There is a distinct difference between bottle-feeding done for the sake of the baby alone and breast-feeding, or breast-nurturing, done for the sake of *both* mother and child. It is this difference, even more than any practical considerations, that makes it easier for bottle-feeding mothers to delegate the task of feeding or holding their children to other people, or even to let a child feed and nurture herself as soon as she is capable. The success of the "teach-them-independence-at-an-early-age" school of child rearing probably lies, in part, in the fact that, for the last several generations, bottle-feeding has been by far the more popular method in infant care.

Women's drive toward intimacy may well be part of a genetic makeup designed to assure that a child is taken care of by her mother. This is sometimes misunderstood. Some mothers may be criticized for being so protective of their children that they are unwilling to have anyone other than themselves—including their husbands—care for their babies. But some women simply have more intense maternal emotions than others. "It was really difficult for me to let go of my baby during the first few months," one mother told me. "It's not that I didn't trust my husband to change him or hold him. I just felt this tremendous feeling that the baby should be in my arms, taken care of by me, be in my aura, so to speak." Many mothers who feel this way find it more difficult to explain, and unless they are speaking with someone who has had similar feelings, they are likely to be misunderstood. But if there is indeed a problem here, it is the misunderstanding of their maternal emotions, not the emotions themselves, that is the cause.

A mother who is in close contact with her baby, and especially one who experiences the mutual benefits of breast-nurturing, often develops such an intimate bond that she "knows" her child's moods, feelings, wants, and needs. This bond benefits both of them. The mother feels good about herself and about motherhood, and her child has proof of her love. For the mother, it fulfills the need for connectedness and intimacy; the baby benefits from having a caretaker and spokesperson who can interpret her needs. It creates a synchronization in which mother and child move in pace with each other. "A mother understands what a child does not say," says a Jewish proverb.

Women who go through a divorce when their children are very young often suffer as a result of our culture's misunderstanding of this connectedness behavior, however. Any number of cases have been brought to my attention in which fathers have sought custody of young (sometimes still breast-feeding) children, on the grounds that their mothers were breast-feeding a child older than two or allowing the children to sleep with them. Sometimes these cases are even brought before the courts as child abuse cases. Since this type of parenting is not the norm in our society and judges may lack understanding of the practice, a mother can face the real possibility of having her children taken away from her. This, warns Ner Littner, M.D., a professor at the Chicago Institute of Psychoanalysis, "can result in a variety of disturbances in the child."[30] And if there were ever an ultimate agony for a mother, whether breast-nurturing or not, it is the forcible taking away of her child. But the stress in our society has been toward a style of parenting that emphasizes detachment, independence, and a child's ability to transfer dependency and love to an inanimate object. Because mothers have become "replaceable," mothers in divorce cases may well find themselves victims of a lack of understanding about the special quality of their bond with their children, writes Dr. Peter Cook.[31]

During the transition time between birth and independence, if a mother nurses her child on demand, nursing becomes associated with nurturing rather than feeding. Women are helped here by their essential gender characteristics, the fact that they have no need to feel in control or have the upper hand when it comes to their children. During this period of intimacy, breast-nurturing helps a mother to tune into her child's needs and feelings, and to realign her priorities in harmony with her child's basic and urgent needs. For most breast-feeding mothers, this is far from the frightening or depersonalizing experience that many men imagine it must be. When her baby cries, the breast-feeding mother's hormones are activated in such a way that it stimulates in her a very real, physical desire to nurse. The nursing that follows is pleasurable for both her and the baby, and satisfies the desire of both for intimacy and bonding. This growing intimacy, in turn, leads to more nursing, and more nursing results in better health for the baby, a feeling of fulfillment for the mother, and, if they remain close to each other enough of the time, the activation of a natural mechanism of child spacing that results in an optimum-length transition period for mother and baby.[32]

Many people who have not had an intimate breast-nurturing experience themselves may think that such a mother's behavior looks like self-denial. In fact, it is usually experienced by the woman as a true enhancement of self. For many mothers, mothering simply feels good. And contrary to the theory that too much closeness is caused by, or can lead to, an unhealthy obsession with keeping a child dependent, long-term breast-feeding mothers (those whose children nurse past the age of three or four) usually cannot tell you when the milk flow stopped or even exactly when the child stopped nursing. It happens so gradually that one day it may just occur to them that the child has not asked to nurse for a while—hardly an indication of obsession. Likewise, one day it will suddenly occur to them that their children are displaying numerous indications of the "independence" that makes so many Western child-rearing experts happy. Well-nurtured bottle-fed babies also display this sense of independence.

And no matter how independent a child becomes, there is always a special link between mother and child, what one mother described as ". . . an invisible umbilical cord, my sixth sense. My sixth sense helps me with decisions," she said, "because I can feel more what my children feel." Dr. Joseph Pearce, author of *The Magical Child*, called this an intuitive sense that is especially strong in mother-child relationships where intimate bonding has been allowed from birth on.[33] As nurturers, mothers develop responsiveness to their children. This means responding not only to their early need for intimacy, but also to their later readiness to go off on their own and become independent. It also means responding to the gender characteristics of the children themselves, such as a daughter's greater need for connectedness or a son's greater need for exploration and physical activity.

According to endocrinologist Estelle Ramey, "Women respond better to stress than men do." Women's bodies produce less adrenaline and cortisol, a stress hormone, than men's do, and the levels of these hormones return more quickly to normal in women.[34] Apparently, not only do women generally feel good about and desire intimacy and connectedness with their children, but their metabolisms are designed to help them deal with the stresses of parenting more effectively than men can.

Even the most stressed-out mothers usually strive for intimacy and connectedness with their children, sometimes to their own detriment. I once attended a reunion of a group of sixteen mothers in their late forties and fifties. It had been about six years since they had all met, and by now their children had left the nest and were well into their own adult lives. One woman after another expressed, through tears, how she was now attempting to put her life back in order after enduring the ravages of alcoholism, verbal abuse, loneliness, or other major stress during her child-rearing years. The women had never spoken about these problems before, and the shock was even greater because in spite of all the agonizing stress, they had been able to give of themselves fully to their children. They had all admired each other's nurturing child rearing in those bygone days. There is something that is so strong in most mothers that, despite tremendous stress and difficulties, they seek above all to fulfill their children's needs. I view this as part of nature's plan to protect children, who otherwise would be threatened with abandonment and have to fend for themselves.

The need for connectedness is so strong in many women that they will endure many things that most men would not, in the hope that they will thereby avoid breaking the bonds to other people that are so important to them. "The recognition of this is apparent in the popularity of the concept of co-dependency," writes Cris Evatt.[35] Just as women's desire for connectedness is often misunderstood, so too is their ability to endure great hardships as they strive to maintain closeness. In fact, the quality that can be labeled co-dependency (and therefore considered a weakness) may in many circumstances be a sign of a characteristically female strength—the ability to nurture in the face of tremendous difficulties. After all, if a woman shows the ability to "hang in there" with her troubled teenager or colicky baby, her strength is considered a blessing. Yet if she shows the same ability in trying to hold together a struggling marriage relationship, she may be accused of weakness for not being assertive enough to "take charge of her life." This is not to say that a woman can, or should, accept whatever abuse is leveled at her. But it seems unfair that a quality that represents great strength can be so completely misunderstood that it is considered a personal failing. And it comes as no surprise that it is a characteristically female strength that is misunderstood; it just shows, once again, how we tend to view male approaches and values as the norm, and female approaches and values as somehow inferior, rather than merely different. (I have been relieved to see, finally, a new movement on the social horizon that questions the national "dependency" on labeling so many of women's behaviors as co-dependent.)

There is a saying that when a baby is born, a mother is born. Before they become mothers, women frequently make promises that will separate them from their future children, before they fully understand the implications of the separation. There is really no way to know ahead of time what it feels like to develop a close, connected bond with one's child. Sometimes women are able to rethink their decisions after the birth. Sometimes, however, they are not, and the result can be painful and difficult. A particularly dramatic case occurred during the 1991 Persian Gulf War, when young mothers who served in the military were sent in unprecedented numbers to serve their country in a distant land, and for an amount of time that was as yet undetermined. I felt a tremendous sympathy for these women, and it called to mind my own experience as a first-time mother.

When I was pregnant with my first child, I had a good job teaching in a Minneapolis music school, and I intended to return to work when my baby was six weeks old. It seemed perfectly plausible. The baby would be old enough to leave with a babysitter; I would be wanting to go back to work. Then my daughter was born. Nothing had prepared me for the powerful changes I felt. They altered my entire value system and completely changed the way I looked at my promise to return to teaching. Taking care of my baby became more important to me than anything else in the world. The feeling startled me, but I followed it, and I did not return to work. From this experience I learned that before a woman becomes pregnant, she has no way of knowing what changes may overcome her; she can only know afterwards. When I thought about young women who had signed up for military service, I wondered, who is going to speak up for them? What are we to tell a woman who, in an innocent, pre-mother state, signed up for the military, with every intention of fulfilling her obligations, but who later became a mother and then, when she is called, has no choice between one of nature's powerful emotions—a mother's need to be with her child—and the contract to serve her country? Is it fair to say to such women, 'You made a well-informed decision,' when in fact they didn't—and couldn't have? As cultural anthropologist David Gutman argued in *Reclaiming Powers*, "Parenthood changes your bed-time, your social life, your idea of what's fun, and importantly, *your sense of what is important*."[36] [Emphasis added.]

Once they become mothers, most women, the world over, naturally and happily give of themselves to hold, cuddle, carry, and breast-nurture their babies, especially if they have the emotional support of others. Most mothers, especially breast-feeding mothers, react with agitation when they hear a child cry, and want to make every attempt to soothe her. Most mothers love and thrive on unhampered intimacy and connectedness with their children, in keeping with the female gender characteristic that seeks to make connections rather than seeking independence, to cooperate rather than to compete. Mothers have the ideal food to meet babies' needs, particularly for the first six months. Women generally can handle stress better than men and can keep several things going at the same time, a critical skill for someone who may have to help more than one child with a task while at the same time cleaning the living room, cooking dinner, doing laundry, letting the dog out, and talking to her husband. This ability for simultaneous multiple involvements, plus a capacity for handling higher levels of stress, is very beneficial in child rearing.

Women's senses are also generally more acute than men's. They have sharper hearing, and are aware of subtle sounds, even when asleep, long before men are. Their smelling and tasting abilities are keener than men's. Women also pick up more quickly on subtle messages of the moods, emotions, and needs of others, and they are more interested in finding out about these things.[37] These are some of the things we know, because we can measure them. We don't as yet know to what extent a mother's aura, her soft skin, her heartbeat, her voice, or other, as-yet-undiscovered, attributes make her ideally suited to care for the infant and young child. And perhaps we never will. As Sir Fred Hoyle, Plumian Professor of Astronomy at Cambridge University, said, "There is no guarantee that the universe is constructed to suit our standards of intelligence."[38] There are some things we may just have to humble ourselves and accept, as expressions of a wisdom we cannot fully understand or explain.

What benefits does the nurturing mother offer her child? Among other things, the child of a nurturing mother:

• Experiences a first love without fear, which serves as a healthy precursor to adult love;

- Develops an ability to trust other people;

- Receives optimum nutrition (breast milk);

- Learns the meaning of intimacy;

- Forms a solid basis for the development of healthy self-esteem;

- Learns the meaning of gentleness;

- Experiences sex identification, male versus female;

- Learns about the joys of life and connectedness with another human being;

- Learns that she is worthwhile and important, and that she has the power to bring about change in her environment;

- May be less vulnerable to SIDS;

- Has a happier infancy and babyhood.

Or, as Elizabeth Barrett Browning so beautifully put it, in her poem *Aurora Leigh*:

> . . . Women know
> The way to rear up children (to be just),
> They know a simple, merry, tender knack
> Of tying sashes, fitting baby-shoes,
> And stringing pretty words that make no sense,
> And kissing full sense into empty words,
> Which things are corals to cut life upon,
> Although such trifles; children learn by such,
> Love's holy earnest in a pretty play
> And get not over-early solemnized,
> But seeing, as in a rose-bush, Love's Divine
> Which burns and hurts not,—not a single bloom,—
> Become aware and unafraid of Love.
> Such good do mothers. . . .[39]

THE TOUCHSTONE

As time goes by, we are certain to learn more about all of the implications of the mother-child bond, for both babies and mothers, from infancy and the younger years until a child grows into independent adulthood. But in the meantime, there must be some touchstone, some truth, to help us decide what best supports the process of rearing healthy children. It is not enough to say that we should listen only to mothers, because of their gender characteristics, for child-rearing advice (although I must admit, as a woman and a mother, I am tempted to); nor should we blindly follow the advice of men just because their beliefs feel right to them. But when husband and wife disagree on what to do, whose opinion should ultimately be followed? Wherein lies the touchstone?

No matter where a child lives—in the United States or India, in Europe or South America; no matter *when* a child lives—3,000 years ago or 60 years ago or today; no matter whether she is an only child or has siblings; and no matter whether her mother holds an outside job or remains at home, a child needs an unhampered nurturing experience with her mother. This is a basic human need that has not changed and will not change. In "A Biosocial Perspective on Parenting," Alice Rossi writes, "In my judgment, by far the wise course [for the future] is to plan and build from the most fundamental root of society in human parenting, and not from the shaky superstructures created by men in that fraction of time in which industrial societies have existed."[40]

It is my strong belief that mother is the touchstone.

People love best when they feel loved. The opposite of being loved is not being hated, as many believe, but being ignored. "There is no greater way to depersonalize another than to speak to him without also listening," wrote Huston Smith in *The Religions of Man*.[41] The experts must not only give advice to mothers, but listen to them as well. Mothers have much to offer. To promote mental health, Dr. Peter Cook writes, we must learn to understand and work with nature rather than against it, especially in the care of infants and young children.[42] This is more easily done if we study the natural experts, mothers.

There are some indications that this process may be beginning. In his newly revised book, *On Becoming a Family*, Dr. T. Berry Brazelton reports that a recent observation of the interaction between a mother and a child caused him to reevaluate one of the long-held tenets of Western child-rearing, that a child needs lavish positive reinforcement to become aware of her accomplishments. Dr. Brazelton tells of a mother in Kenya who was showing her young child how to perform a task. After the demonstration she sat back and remained silent, except for a quiet, "You can do it," as he accomplished the first stage of the task and proceeded to the next stage. After a while, Dr. Brazelton noticed that, even though the mother remained silent, the child displayed excitement and increased interest in the task. This was very different from the American mothers he had observed, who "routinely demonstrated the task one step at a time, talking about each step in an instructive manner as they went along." In a subtle way, he noted, the American mothers made each achievement not quietly the child's own, but a reflection of their enthusiasm. "Depending on how it is used," he observes, "[enthusiastic positive reinforcement] can be very manipulative." Dr. Brazelton concludes that, as compared to the Kenyan mother, "it was obvious that U.S. mothers were more controlling with their reinforcement and the opportunity for the baby to realize his own autonomous achievement was diluted." The Kenyan child, on the other hand, proceeded uninterrupted, at his own pace, to explore the task from one level of success to the next.[43]

I sense a similarity here to the well-nurtured baby who

is allowed to wean herself and grow at her own speed, without any particular prodding or applause, but simply at her own rate. Was the Kenyan mother displaying the nurturing mothering characteristic that provides a secure background, but does not need to push or challenge? Perhaps there is a correlation between the male desire for achievement, competition, and expansion, which is simultaneously reflected in and reinforced by our culture's male dominance in child rearing, and our having become conditioned to think that positive reinforcement is critical to a baby's becoming aware of her accomplishments and developing self-esteem. Dr. Brazelton's observation seems to point to yet another manifestation of the differences between how men and women approach child rearing, and how the male-oriented approach has influenced our perceptions.

A word of caution is in order here. This book is meant to explore the differences between men and women in their approach to child rearing, and to emphasize the importance of recognizing the validity of women's values. I do *not* intend to imply that if children are just raised according to maternal feelings, they will grow up without any problems. Any number of books on child rearing give the impression that if a reader simply follows a prescribed formula, he or she can magically raise children without suffering any of the unpleasant consequences experienced by those who are ignorant of it. Many books convey the subtle (and sometimes not so subtle) message that if a child does not "turn out right," it is the fault of the parents—especially the mother—because they failed to follow the formula properly. Mother-blaming has been an unfortunate, and perhaps unintentional, byproduct of many otherwise well-meaning child-rearing books.

There are no magic formulas. Rearing a child lovingly does not mean that you will have control over how much happiness she will experience in her teenage or adult years. We must love our children, wholly and fully and unconditionally, but *not* with the mistaken idea that this will protect them from going astray as teenagers, or that it will cloak us all in such loveliness that no unhappiness, pain, anger, doubt, fear, or distress can ever disturb the equilibrium of our family. We are all subject to influences beyond our control that can create detours, stresses, and unhappiness for which we are ill-prepared. Life is difficult. And love is not a magic wand. But love, and everything it represents, provides the best basis for dealing with life, with all its potential problems. We all need all the love we can get, and especially a mother's inherent love at the very beginning: a love that is nurturing but not smothering; a love that holds us close but is prepared to let go; a love that is given for the benefit of the child, not for the mother's own benefit.

The unjust experimentation in enforcing premature independence in children must come to an end. It is for the benefit of children, after all, that nature has given them caretakers who are female, with their unique nurturing and interdependent characteristics. Of course, there is no conclusive data that proves a child needs her own biological mother to fulfill all of her needs. Fathers, foster parents, aunts, and others can all nurture a child, and they all have their places in the lives of children. Children can be reared well by any of them, even without a mother. Life is too precious to have to rely on only one source. But of all the people available to an infant or young child, a baby's own mother, with her gender characteristic nurturing approach, is best able to meet most of her needs, most of the time, and current research continues to support this.

A final question: Who, then, should we regard as the experts and role models for early child rearing? I believe that mothers are the ones we should look to. Just as we would ask women, not men, about menstruation, so we should ask mothers about mothering. And what kind of mothering am I talking about? I believe the answer is the type of mothering that most closely follows the ways of mothers throughout the ages and throughout the world; a type of close, connected child rearing that fulfills both the short-term and long-term needs of mother and child. Unfortunately, this is a rarity in our culture today. Mothers who cannot or who choose not to be full-time mothers may feel hurt or left out because I consider full-time breast-nurturing to be the ideal approach. I know well that most mothers, no matter what their circumstances, truly do the best they can, and for this they are to be given our full support and credit. But still I believe we cannot ignore a certain guideline, set forth by nature, that points to the full-time, breast-nurturing mother as the source of wisdom on early child rearing.

Then what about men? If women are the true experts, where do men—whether child-rearing experts or fathers—fit in? Are they even necessary? I say yes, very much so. We will examine the importance of men in child rearing in the following chapter.

Chapter 6

The Importance of the Encouraging Father

While mother is the primary *nurturer* in the family, father takes the role of the primary *encourager*, of independence, achievement, and ambition. Where a mother might say to a child climbing a tree, "Be careful. Don't go too high," a father is apt to say, "I'm right here. Can you go one limb higher?" This is a natural outgrowth of his essential gender characteristics, which emphasize expansion, challenges, achievement, seeking a higher position, and encouraging the development of independence. Fathers tend to invest more than mothers do in their children's ability to perform well in the world, and take pride in their children's accomplishments there.

A mother fulfills her child's need for deep intimacy, especially in the early years, and especially with her daughter as she grows into womanhood. A father provides the encouragement his child needs to reach out, especially as the child grows into greater independence and especially with his son, as he learns to function in the hierarchical society of men.

Both mother and father are vitally important in the child's life. Either can, if needed, fill in for the other. However, each has his or her own special place in a child's life, not only individually, as parents to the child, but also together, as parents *of* the child—that is, as a man and woman who can show the child what loving, committed family relationships are all about. Such a mother and father complement, support, and respect each other, creating a harmony that forms the support system of a child's life. Although in many families this kind of ideal is never achieved, it is nevertheless a harmony that most couples wish for when they marry, and that nearly all parents wish to create for their children. It is this hope that gives many parents the encouragement to keep working toward a better future.

A presentation to a UNICEF seminar on early childhood development stated: "It has long been accepted that good health and nutrition support the psychological and social development of the young child. Less widely recognized are the more recent findings that developmentally sensitive interaction with a child, namely *interaction which satisfies the child's need to grow socially, psychologically, and cognitively*, has a direct and measurable impact on the physical health of the child. While the implications of these interaction effects are of considerable importance for the health and well-being of children, *they have been seriously neglected in development planning.*"[1] [Emphasis added.] The direct and constant interaction of parents and children has, unfortunately, been undermined in our society, and the role of the father especially has suffered. A great deal of emphasis has been placed on the importance of the schools—a source of influence that comes from outside the family—in a child's development. This is often done at the expense of recognizing the influences on the child from within the family, and especially the influence of the father.

WHAT A FATHER IS

As a child grows and expands his world away from his mother, he needs another human being who is equally trustworthy and encourages the development of independence, making him ready for the transition to adulthood. This where a father plays one of his most vital roles, and his inherent male gender characteristics make him particularly well suited to it. In the security of his father's love, a child receives the encouragement, support, and trust he needs to venture out and grow up. This is what Margaret Mead must have meant when she wrote, "... the child grows toward the father."[2] And this is what Jean Liedloff described in her observation of a preliterate tribe: "[The child's] mother cares for him simply because he is there; his existence is reason enough to guarantee her love. Her unconditional acceptance remains constant as his father emerges as an important figure interested in his developing social behavior and his advance toward independence. The father's constant love maintains the same character as the mother's but has an overlay of approval contingent upon the performance of the child. Thus nature insures both stability and incentive toward sociality."[3]

When a child is born, he is naturally and totally dependent on his mother. Gradually, as he grows older, his father encourages him to stretch his horizons and face the challenges of life, until the child reaches adulthood and the cycle begins all over again. The father is thus the person who can challenge the child, in an environment of love and safety, to try new things and to grow up. As we have seen, over the last 100 years or so many Western child-rearing experts have been encouraging *mothers* to rear their children according to a male-oriented approach. Most of these "experts" had little or no awareness of the validity of maternal emotions. Fathers generally could relate to the advice of these men (and for the most part, they were men) and enforced it in the home. Ironically, however, by insist-ing that their wives follow characteristically male ap-proaches, they began to lose their own special place in the child-rearing process. In addition, the feminist movement in this country, in its eagerness to assure women that divorced or single mothers could indeed raise healthy children, actually discouraged many men from fulfilling their role at home. (It may have discouraged some women as well, by implying that children would do just as well in daycare centers while their mothers went off to vie for positions in the hierarchical business world.) The move-ment was so intent on achieving the legitimate goal of equality in the workplace that it began to expand the principle of strict equality into people's private behavior as well, according to writer Sally Quinn.[4] The message that a woman can do anything a man can do seemed to many men to say also, by implication, that men had nothing special to offer. As a result, they felt devalued, deprived of the importance they had once had, and unsure about how to behave or relate to their families.

Of course, for many mothers, the move to the workplace was simply a matter of economic necessity. More women than ever before are rearing children without the benefit of a partner, and since the 1980s, especially, many families have found that it takes two incomes (and sometimes more) just to afford the basic necessities. Also, for many women, having a career outside the home is the only way to feel that they are exercising their intellects and energies. These are very complex issues. For many people, the har-monious traditional family unit is no more than a nostalgic ideal. Yet research shows that—despite all the social and economic changes our society has undergone—it remains the goal that most people hope to achieve, probably be-cause the unity and support of a healthy, complete family fulfill a deep, basic human need.

Research showing that a child raised predominantly by his father will be more outspoken, less afraid of strangers, and have a better-developed learning ability than a child reared only by his mother is often cited to "prove" that men can raise children as well as women can. Other research is cited to "prove" the superiority of mother-only families. Sometimes, it is women who claim that men can be just as good as mothers at child rearing—often, following their female gender characteristics, out of a desire to keep everybody happy and not to hurt men's feelings. Sometimes it is men who say, "We can be just as effective at rearing children"—but what they really mean is, "Don't tell me I can't do this. I am just as capable as any woman, if not more so." Displaying a typical male characteristic, they are refusing to accept a lower hierarchical position. What all of these arguments miss, however, is that, in general, children develop best of all when *both* a mother and a father raise them. Child rearing should not be a contest. Ideally, it should be a process in which both parents fulfill their individual roles, unique to their own gender, for the benefit of their children and the family.

While men can certainly raise children well, they are *not* mothers. Nor should they be. Fathers should be celebrated for what they are—men, with typically male gender characteristics—and for their own particular importance in the lives of their children and families. To argue that mothers and fathers should be interchangeable is to deny the real and important differences between men and women, mothers and fathers. These differences should be honored, not ignored or rejected. If both men and women would give their spouses respect for their place in the family and their children's lives, and if they were given support and credit for being good and valuable as women/mothers or men/fathers, they could focus on what is best for their children rather than on themselves. As columnist Mona

Charen wrote, "Men will accept their position as fathers, not by making them a pale substitute of mother, but by being appreciated by our culture."[5]

If children generally learn the meaning of intimacy, gentleness, and an orientation toward other people from their mothers, it is from their fathers that they learn the meaning of independence, autonomy, taking on challenges, channelling and controlling aggression, and an orientation toward learning about the outside world. The Greeks understood and praised this positive male energy, according to poet Robert Bly. "They called it Zeus energy, which encompasses intelligence, robust health, compassionate decisiveness, good will, generous leadership," he writes.[6] Bly points out that throughout history, all the great cultures (except ours) have lived with and preserved images of positive male energy. In our society, however, manliness is often associated with violence and oppression rather than anything positive. There are other men today who lament this state of affairs. David Blankenhorn, president of the New York-based Institute for American Values, writes, "I want to teach my son to be a good man and a good father. But when I look around for help and reinforcement in that crucial task, I see a culture that, at its best, communicates confusion, fears and anxiety on the entire subject of what it means for a boy to become a man. At its worst, I see our culture as actively hostile to the entire enterprise."[7]

We live in a world where men tell women how to rear infants and young children. At the same time, many women want men to be more gentle (that is, more like women), while they themselves work at becoming more aggressive (that is, like men) so that they can fight their way to the top in the competitive working world. The immediate connection between mothers and children, through pregnancy and birth, still gives women a basic feeling of their role in the family. But fathers are lost in a sort of no-man's land (no pun intended) and don't know where they fit in. "Fathers are curious people," writes Christopher Hallowell in *Father to the Man*. ". . . [They] pop in and out of young lives, often sharing a reputation for being distant and preoccupied with their own affairs."[8] Some fathers, feeling that their only function is to provide a paycheck, quietly dissolve into the background and say, with a shrug of the shoulder, "What am I needed for, anyway?"

Well, come back, Dad. The family needs you.

THE FATHER-CHILD BOND

How soon a father is included in his child's world depends on how close he is to his family. In some cultures, the father's involvement begins during pregnancy, with specific taboos and responsibilities he must observe as soon as pregnancy is evident.[9] In our Western culture, many fathers begin to feel a sense of involvement when they are present during birth, especially if they support their wives through the birthing process. Like mothers, fathers can bond with their infants. At the moment of birth, seeing their own offspring emerge into the world, many men experience an overwhelming feeling of love for their children and for their wives. Fathers who have this experience with their infants usually find it to be one of the most wonderful, life-awakening experiences in their lives. "The feeling of bonding is incredible," one father told me. "It just blew me away."

Some men feel that fatherhood is less a matter of biology than of a cultural script, and that fatherhood is something that must be learned.[10] Such a man may not feel an overwhelming love for his child during the first few weeks. Other men feel that fatherhood is a biologically-based experience for men, just as it is for women. But whereas women's hormones are activated during pregnancy and childbirth and set maternal instincts in motion, paternal emotions must be evoked by the child himself.

Studies show that the ability to provide nurturing attention and care for children is genderless. This research indicates not only how crucial nurturing is in a child's development, but also how good men can be at nurturing.[11] And infants have a wonderful way of eliciting nurturing feelings from nearly anyone who comes in close contact with them. However, in general, men are less frequently drawn to children than women are, even when they are equally available to each other. A study of ten different cultures revealed, though, that once bonding has taken place, men's level of interaction with their children becomes more similar to that of women.[12] Studies further indicate that the more a father interacts with his offspring, the gentler and kinder he is toward his children.[13]

In general, fathers are likely to be more drawn to boy babies than to girl babies, and to become more directly involved in taking care of them. From the very beginning, men look at, talk to, and touch boys more, and this intensifies as the boys grow older.[14] Some men do not feel at ease connecting closely with infants, but prefer to wait until a child is a bit older. They acquire the title of father sooner than they feel ready to fulfill the role. This does not necessarily keep them from developing a loving and caring relationship with their children later, however. Robert Bly wrote of his own experience, "Many men—myself included—have found inside [themselves] an ability to nurture that didn't appear until it was called for."[15]

In "Parameters of the Adult-Male Child," Wade Macky reports that while male parenting behavior is similar to female parenting behavior, women initiate contact with their children more often and maintain close contact longer.[16] This is hardly surprising; it follows female and male gender characteristics. But intimate bonding has positive effects on men, too. Fathers who establish an early bond with their children find it easier to feel closer to them. Dr. William Sears believes that a father, stimulated by his child's reaction to contact with him, experiences a feeling of "rightness" that makes it easier for him to practice "involved fathering." This he describes as "a type of parenting which is an uninterrupted, nurturing relationship, specifically attuned to a child's needs as he passes from one developmental stage to the next."[17] As one father said, "Once you have experienced that bonding, that love between you and your child, you're hooked." It is powerful.

The father-child bond is as important to the health and harmony of the family relationship as the mother-child bond and the bond between husband and wife, and is equally deserving of protection and support. All of these family ties stand to benefit greatly if a mother and father can both recognize their own feelings. Some men feel displaced, unimportant, or uninvolved after the arrival of a child, a feeling some male doctors have referred to as "being in competition" with the child for the mother's attention. No one, and certainly not a husband, wants to play second fiddle in his own home. The adjustment that comes with having a child takes effort and understanding. Instead of allowing misunderstandings about each other's feelings to create a rift, I would suggest that both partners explore and acknowledge their own—and each other's—emotional responses, while at the same time adopting an attitude of, "How can I be of greatest help in our relationship and our family?"

In general, we all tend to be better off when we are able to shift our focus away from ourselves. It usually makes us feel better, often helps us to be more productive, and may have other unanticipated benefits as well. "My husband has become more willing to be a father to our children since I made it a point not to interfere with his relationship with them," wrote one mother. This in turn enhanced the spousal relationship between the two of them. This shift in focus may pose a somewhat greater challenge for men than women, though. According to Cris Evatt's research, the ability to focus on other people's needs usually comes more easily to women than to men, who tend to be more self-focused. In *Men, Women and Relationships,* John Gray says: "A man's biggest difficulty is to overcome his tendency to be self-absorbed."[18] However, I would say that this is not so much a difficulty that must be overcome as a characteristic to become aware of. Self-focus is an inherent male gender characteristic, and it has its positive aspects. Only if it causes a serious problem should it be labeled a difficulty.

In families with close father-child bonds, women see their husbands relating to their children with warmth and affection, and can sense their reciprocal joy and involvement. This often makes a wife feel closer to her husband, which enhances the quality of their marriage. And once a father has established his own close relationship with his offspring, he is less likely to feel as if he is an outsider or, at best, a mother substitute. It is difficult for some husbands to see their wives' attention drawn to a young child so much of the time, both day and might. By establishing his own relationship with his child as a father, a man is more likely to feel like an integral part of the family. At the same time, he is usually better able to accept his wife's emotions as a mother, and to suffer less from the jealous feeling that the baby is upstaging him. A close relationship between father and child also communicates to the child that father is an important part of the family because of who he is, not just because of the material things he can provide. And interestingly, a study of ninety nonindustrial societies has found that "the more men are involved in child rearing, the higher the status of women in the society. Father-child relationships have a significant effect on female status."[19] This may not apply perfectly to our industrialized society, but it does point out that when men are intimately involved with the family, they are more likely to be friends with their wives and children, and mothers are likely to receive greater recognition for their contributions, both as mothers and as intelligent human beings.

THE FATHER AS ROLE MODEL

It is important for a child to have the chance to observe how his father and mother treat each other, how they treat their children, and how, both together and separately, they treat life. In *Creative Parenting*, Dr. William Sears writes: "Modeling means providing behavior that is perceived by your child as genuine, consistent and desirous of imitation."[20] It is through exposure to role models that children learn how to treat their friends and, later, to relate to their spouses, parent their own children, and cope with life's difficulties. From a parental role model, children can learn the basic value of commitment, and come to understand that commitment and love are sources of fulfillment, not oppression. They can learn that a man and a woman, though in some ways so very different, can achieve great fullness of life within a loving and respectful relationship.

Most parents, after all, wish to transmit their own values to their children. Being able to pass on our ideas about life to our children helps us to answer a question many people ask as they grow older: "What value has my life had?" It is important for parents to demonstrate to children what it means to help and be helped by your partner in times of stress, to share responsibilities, to take turns, to go out of your way for another person, to provide needed advice and encouragement. Children benefit tremendously from seeing a relationship in which one partner turns to the other in times of both trouble and joy, a relationship in which the partners work together, giving and receiving within a committed partnership, for the enrichment of both and of each other. This does not mean that life will always be a bed of roses. Life is difficult. It has its periods of stress, tragedy, sadness, and anger. But children who learn from their parents that while life is difficult, its difficulties are not usually insurmountable, can go on to become active, self-confident participants in life.

Fathers can be very good at communicating that message to children. My own father was instrumental in teaching me that lesson, and my way of honoring him (and my mother also) for that great gift has been to try to pass it on to my own children. Many people find themselves unable to accept that life is by nature difficult, and "moan more or less incessantly, noisily or subtly, about the enormity of their problems, their burdens, and their difficulties as if life were generally easy, as if life should be easy. They voice their belief, noisily or subtly, that their difficulties represent a unique kind of affliction that should not be and that has somehow been especially visited upon them, or else upon their families, their tribe, their class, their nation, their race or even their species, and not upon others," as M. Scott Peck writes in *The Road Less Traveled*.[21]

From the models their parents provide, children can learn that even though life is difficult, these difficulties are problems to be solved, not to be bemoaned or passed off as the fault of someone else. Since an orientation toward problem-solving is a characteristically male trait, fathers can play a critical role here. Role modeling is a lifelong assignment, and a serious one. Children will remember vividly the roles their fathers played.

THE FATHER AS PROTECTOR

Most of us have, at one time or another, conjured up an image of fathers as the men who stood guard at the mouths of caves to protect their families against wild beasts and dangerous intruders. It is easy for us now to assume that since we no longer have such perils lurking about, fatherly protection is no longer needed. This is seriously demoralizing to many men, however, and makes them feel unnecessary and unappreciated.

The instinct to protect those they love from danger is a strong part of the gender characteristic makeup of many men. It makes them feel good to know that they are providing safety for their families. One man told me that the emotion that surprised him the most after his divorce was the empty feeling that he was no longer able to fulfill this urge to protect. A man in his sixties, whose children had married and moved out, said that what he missed most was being able to put his big arms around his kids and "protect" them. It's true that for the most part we no longer face danger from four-footed, fanged, and furred creatures, but there are still many "wild beasts" that fathers can help defend against.

What are some of the modern-day wild beasts? Stress, for one. Many women who choose to stay at home, for instance, experience great stress as the result of both economic pressure and the pull of messages from our society, which glorifies the woman who works outside the home. Many women who do work outside the home experience stress because they must work even though they would prefer not to, and feel guilty about not being home with their children. Fathers, by being actively involved in family life, giving their wives support, and appreciating their contributions, can help to ease some of this stress. Women need to know that they are appreciated and recognized for their intelligence and who they are as individuals, as well as for mothering and homemaking. They need to know

that their husbands, at least, don't look down on mothering as an inferior occupation, and that they don't consider
men's contributions to the family to be superior to
women's. Men can help their wives find solutions that
affirm the worth and balance the needs of everyone in the
family. Women who do not need to work outside the home
for financial reasons may discover that doing volunteer
work, which usually entails a more flexible schedule, gives
them the mental stimulation they need, as well as tremendous satisfaction. Others may find work that they can do
at home, fulfilling the need for additional income and
mental stimulation, as well as for being at home with
children. With the electronics revolution that has made it
possible to connect anyone, anywhere with virtually anyone else, as well as society's growing acceptance of at-
home businesses, this is becoming an increasingly viable
way to meet a family's need for income as well as children's need for full-time parenting. Finding ways to make
these or other solutions work can help relieve some of the
stresses felt by families today. Fathers can play a very
supportive part in making this happen.

A father can also protect his family physically. David
Blankenhorn asks, "When a prowler breaks into the house,
who goes downstairs?" Most women feel a great deal safer
when there is a man in the house, or with a man beside them
when they walk down a dark street. Also, tasks requiring
physical strength—moving furniture, bringing in bags of
groceries, shoveling snow, taking out heavy cans of gar-
bage—will always be with us, and with the help of a man,
they remain manageable tasks, rather than becoming insurmountable obstacles. "The feminist movement has not yet
been able to obliterate the physical strength of men," Mona
Charen wrote in the *Savannah News*.[22]

There are any number of other wild beasts out there as
well for a father to deal with: the sexy clothes his twelve-

year-old daughter wants to wear; harrassing telephone calls; malfunctioning appliances; flat tires; bills that need to be paid; the stress of a crying baby after a restless night; fights between siblings that need the deep voice of authority from Dad to call a halt. It may sound old-fashioned to talk about fathers as protectors, but there are still many things we need protection from, and fathers are uniquely qualified to provide that protection.

THE FATHER AS SUPPORTER

In addition to protecting his family, a father can provide invaluable support for his wife and children. One aspect of this, of course, is financial. As we have seen, babies and young children who receive a great deal of continuous nurturing are much more likely to grow up to be emotionally healthy adults. And despite everything we hear about the joys of the working woman, most mothers say they *want* to be at home to care for the family, especially when their children are very young. A survey reported by the *Los Angeles Times* showed that 80 percent of working mothers would choose to stay at home with their children if they could afford it. A *Washington Post* poll concluded that 62 percent of working mothers would prefer to stay at home specifically because they felt their children suffered as a result of the demands work placed on them.[23] Not only do they wish to stay home for the sake of the children, but many women say they truly enjoy making a home, a nest, for their family—another expression of their nurturing gender characteristic.

In order to do this, however, a woman needs someone (ideally her husband) who can provide for her and their children. "For a woman to adequately discharge her responsibilities to her child(ren), she needs a good man by her side," writes Dr. Harold Voth, senior psychiatrist with

the Menninger Foundation.[24] The father used to be called
the "breadwinner." This is a very good term. Without a
father to provide financial security, a mother cannot provide full-time nurturing care for their children. And despite all the changes in the roles and relationships of men
and women, in a recent survey on the meaning of masculinity in our society, most people—both men and
women—said that being a good provider is the single most
important element of what it means to be a man.

But support is not only a matter of money. A father can
also give his family emotional support. If a wife knows
that her husband sees her as a nurturing, competent, sensitive caregiver—in short, a good mother—she is much
more able to cope with the stresses of child care, hurt
feelings, too little sleep, and the host of daily frustrations
that come with keeping a home. Studies have shown that
in families in which fathers are supportive of mothers, the
relationships between mothers and children are more
likely to be close and affectionate.[25] When a day at home
or at the office has been particularly disastrous, nothing is
as wonderful for a mother as hearing a supportive comment from her husband and having him pitch in and help
her, or at least provide an understanding ear.

A father can give his children crucial emotional support
simply by being involved in their lives. A father's interest
in and approval of their efforts conveys a powerful message to children. When a father compliments or congratu-
lates his child on a job well done, makes the time to attend
the school play or a Little League game—or just listens to
a child's troubles and says, "I love you"—he is telling the
child that he matters, that his concerns and achievements
are important. These are essential building blocks of family bonds and a child's self-esteem.

Fathers can also support their families by enforcing
discipline. Children of all ages need and want the security

of boundaries as they develop and, yes, test themselves against those limits. It is often easier for a man to stick with rules and be authoritative, because of his inherently hierarchical view of the world, whereas women are more likely to try to talk things out. Talking things out is often a very good approach, but there are times when talking doesn't work. Older children especially may need a stricter approach to maintaining and learning discipline. Many mothers have told me that Dad's request or warning usually gets a quicker response than Mom's, an observation that is borne out by research. For example, a study on the effects of divorce on children found that children are more likely to obey their fathers than their mothers, whether the parents are married to one another or not.[26]

Research has indicated that children who grow up with nurturing mothers who satisfy their immediate needs as babies and young children, and fathers who encourage them and enforce adherence to household rules, grow up to be more capable of delaying gratification, and to have greater respect for others and for order. Respect for the father is especially enhanced if he is involved in child rearing from birth on. According to Dr. Sears, early involvement helps a trusting relationship to develop between father and child, which makes it easier for the father to discipline the child later on. "Being affectionate allows father to be more firm about setting limits," he writes.[27]

FATHERS AND SONS

Only a father (or, if need be, another male mentor) can provide a rich, confident model of manhood for a boy as he leaves the intimate world of his mother. "Both male and female cells carry marvelous music, but the son needs to resonate to the masculine frequency as well as to the female frequency," writes poet Robert Bly.[28] Research has shown that between the ages of three and five, boys begin to disengage themselves from the female world. Their play becomes more focused on rules, strength, challenges, power, and achievement. They are more apt to begin exerting their masculine gender characteristic of hierarchical maneuvering and boast of accomplishments, often their fathers' as well as their own, as in, "My daddy drives a bigger truck than your daddy."

Some research seems to indicate that boys nurse a few months longer, on average, than girls do. It is almost as if a boy needs this extra dose of maternal intimacy before he launches into the challenging, independent masculine world. As he begins to experiment in this brave new world, he still needs, at times, to return to the reassuring intimacy of his mother's arms. But if he has developed a close and trusting relationship with his father, he will often feel just as reassured in his father's arms, and will probably surprise his mother one day by asking that "Daddy do it."

As a boy grows older, if the trusting relationship between him and his father continues, he can develop a sense of respect, of admiration for his parent. He may even consider his father a hero. This paves the way for the development of a healthy sense of self-esteem in the boy. The youth may make every attempt to emulate his father.

Because it is always easier to feel more at ease with someone with whom you are familiar, a father may draw away from his children if he feels unsure in his relationship with them. Likewise, children may fear their fathers if they do not know them. If such fear is never dealt with properly, a child may grow up with unresolved feelings of fear, strangeness, hurt, or anger about this man who is his father. He may carry these emotions over into his relationships with other men. Recently, several popular books have explored the subject of unresolved fear and the anger of adult sons toward their fathers. Books such as Bly's *Iron John* and

Finding our Fathers by Samuel Osherson leave no doubt that some men carry throughout their lives the tragic weight of the boy child's unfulfilled need to know his father and his father's love. For some of these men, healing finally begins when they become fathers themselves and actively participate in rearing their own sons. "It's so natural for me to hug and kiss my son and tell him I love him," said one young father as he sat with his three-year-old straddling his lap. "But I still find it hard to do more than shake hands with my old man, with whom I feel an uncomfortable distance, even though he is my dad."

Of course, fathers need not necessarily hug and kiss their sons a lot to establish a close bond with them. This point was eloquently brought home by Howard Sivertson in a book about his childhood on Isle Royal in Lake Superior. His father was a fisherman, and by the age of twelve the author actively participated in the daily hard work. He writes:

> The "interpersonal relationships" jargon we hear today didn't exist when I was a child. My father didn't tiptoe into my shack early each morning to gently request that we spend some quality time together in a meaningful way. Before dawn, I heard the screen door slam on the family cabin, followed by the sound of heavy boots crunching on gravel, then the thud of my dad's ham-like fist on the side of my shack. I was half-dressed in my cold clothes, still wet from yesterday, by the time he grunted, "Let's go!" and crunched on down the path to the fish house and the waiting boat.[29]

But it is clear to the reader that the bond between father and son was strong, genuine, and solid, and that is what is so crucial to a boy's development.

Clinical studies and anthropological investigations seem to confirm the process by which boys separate from their mothers in search of the meaning of their maleness. In this process, the father or a strong male substitute is irreplaceable. He enables the son to separate from the mother and begin to identify with his masculine feelings from a male point of view, says David Blankenhorn.[30] His mother may encourage his masculine development, but she can only do this from her perspective as a woman. Her son may admire her for this, but he will never feel at home with it.[31] According to Rita Kramer's research, a boy's "identification with a strong and confidently masculine father who is admired by a mother who encourages the boy's identification with his father's masculine traits rather than her own feminine ones is the sine qua non of the development of masculinity in a boy."[32]

Sons need to undergo a psychological separation from their mothers and an identification and bonding with their fathers, writes Osherson in *Finding Our Fathers*. They especially need to learn from their fathers about normal, healthy emotions, that it is okay to cry, to be gentle and caring. One man lamented of his fatherless upbringing, "It was not until my early adulthood that I realized how desperately I wanted to know, from a man, that it was all right to be afraid. Women will tell you it's okay. But in the back of my mind I always thought, 'That's okay for girls; they're sissies anyway.' When I learned from a man [that] it was okay, I suddenly became aware of many more of my emotions."

Boys need their fathers as role models to learn about independence and hierarchy. These can both be very fine things. Hierarchy creates order out of complexity and can spur people to higher levels of achievement. Challenging and conquering life's difficult situations can lead to feeling alive and exuberant, especially for boys and men.

Aggressiveness seems to be a universal male trait, and

as with all drives varies in intensity in different individuals. The acceptable manner in which this aggression may be expressed or acted out differs from society to society, but it is from men within his society that a boy can learn how to channel his aggression in an acceptable way. This is why fathers are needed. They can best teach their sons how to channel their characteristically male aggression into healthy and useful outlets, through teaching, playing, and challenging each other. This does not mean encouraging "hypermasculinity" through either mistreatment or modeling over-aggressive behavior. In fact, overly aggressive parental role-modeling may actually interfere with a boy's developing gender identification and make him search continually for the true meaning of his masculinity. Likewise, a boy who reaches his teenage years without having a strong, positive male role model in his life may need to make up his own definition of what it means to be a man. He is quite likely to fall under the ever-present influences of television, movies, and advertising, and end up engaging in promiscuous sex, joining a gang, drinking, and/or smoking "like a man." Ironically, according to some sociologists, it is the absence of a father that can lay the foundation for a boy becoming involved in self-destructive or delinquent "hypermasculine" behavior.

Blankenhorn goes so far as to say that "fathers are the enemy of crime."[33] He says, "If we are seeking the identity of the rapist, the hater of women, the occupant of jail cells, research shows that we look first to the tragedy of boys growing up without fathers. . . . I see a direct link between the senseless violence on our streets and a generation of young males raised without the love, discipline and guidance of a father."[34] Thomas Sowell, Ph.D., senior fellow at the Hoover Institution in Stanford, California, and a supporter of the role of fathers in the lives of sons, wrote in *Forbes*: "If facts carried as much weight as rhetoric, we would have to recognize that parental influence has proved to be much more effective than condoms, sex education and school based clinics."[35] On January 9, 1992, Dr. Louis W. Sullivan, then Secretary of Health and Human Services, spoke to the inaugural meeting of the Council on Families in America, and said, "Though our society is only beginning to recognize it, the greatest family issue of our era is fatherlessness—male absence from family life. . . . Generally speaking, children missing a parent are more vulnerable." He cited as examples:

- Children without fathers at home are five times more likely to be poor and twice as likely to drop out of school.

- Approximately 70 percent of juveniles in long-term correctional facilities did not live with their fathers growing up.

Obviously, not all children whose fathers are not around develop serious problems. Conversely, not all sons whose fathers are available to them will grow up without problems. Many other factors go into rearing healthy children: environment, education, nutrition, personality, social circumstances, economic conditions. But in general, research seems to indicate that the more a father participates in child rearing and the more time he spends with his children, the greater the chance for stability in the child's life and psychological makeup.

When a boy has a good relationship with his father, it seems to be easier for him to be affectionate with his mother. A study conducted at Memphis State University and the University of Missouri found that mother-son relationships were much warmer and more affectionate in households where the father was present.[36] In such households, there is less of the awkwardness or ugliness from teenage sons toward their mothers that Robert Bly says is present all over the country. Kathyrn Ramp, an associate professor of human development and family life at the University of Kansas, said that when fathers have not been involved, or are not even around, "there often is exaggerated conflict with the mother. The kids get to be 13 or 14, they're bigger than Mom, and they're off. She's no match for them. There's no one who can deal with them whose respect they have."

When fathers participate in the child-rearing process, it is easier for sons to experience an initiation into the adult male world, whether it takes the form of a camping trip, working on a car together, competing in a sport, or any other rite of passage that serves the same purpose. This symbolic breaking of his tie with his mother brings pride to the boy as he is accepted in the male world as a man. He can know where he stands and so doesn't need to struggle with self-identity. According to an article in *Mothering* magazine, small groups across the country are responding to this need by organizing initiation rites for their sons. Author Bernard Weiner notes, "There is a ravenous hunger in our times: Men and women of all ages and interests are yearning for meaningful ritual."[37]

This is why I think it is wise of the Boy Scouts of America not to allow girls into their clubs. I admire the spirit of the girls who, from time to time, challenge the Scouts' policy. But I believe we should also think of the boys, many of whom are growing up without the male mentors and role models they so desperately need. Boys need to experience initiation into adulthood surrounded by men. They need to learn manliness from men, ideally from their own fathers first and later from other male leaders and mentors. There is every indication that boys benefit greatly from a specific, designated time alone with their male role models. As Phyllis Theroux said in *Night Lights*, "Small boys learn to be large men in the presence of large men who care about small boys."[38]

FATHERS AND DAUGHTERS

Fathers have an important role to play in encouraging their daughters to grow into healthy young women and to realize their femininity. "How a father treats his daughter," Rita Kramer writes, "his image of what is attractive in a female . . . is a great influence . . . in shaping female behavior."[39] In the safety of her father's arms, a girl can learn to trust men, which will have a lasting effect on her relationships with men, especially her spouse, later in life. According to Judith Wallerstein, executive director of the Center for the Family in Transition in Corte Madera, California, girls whose fathers practice "involved fathering" are much less likely to engage in premarital or promiscuous sex or to become involved with older men than are girls who have not experienced their fathers' loving care from childhood on. Of the latter, she writes, "Trading sex for closeness now, they want to be held and cuddled by their older lover, as if they are trying to recapture, or experience for the first time, the physical nearness that very young children seek by crawling into daddy's lap."[40] When a girl has a good relationship with a loving father, she may look for his traits in a husband, too, rather than simply settling for the first man who pays attention to her.

Because fathers tend to encourage their children to take on challenges, daughters receive from them recognition of their achievements and the encouragement to excel. When my children (both girls) brought home report cards, I would always ask them, "Do you feel good about your work?" Their father, with equal enthusiasm, would ask, "What grade did you get?" When one of my daughters told me about a friend who had received a higher mark on a project, I replied, "But is she nice?" To me, being a good friend was much more important than getting a high mark on a project, as long as my daughter had done her best. Hearing this, the husband of a friend commented, "What I would have said is, 'Let's see what we can do so that you can get a higher mark, too.'" In other words, he would encourage her to challenge the other girl, with the intent of doing better, achieving more. And this is good.

Dr. Louise Bates Ames tells fathers to get involved with their daughters from birth on—to hold them, carry them, do things with them—so that they get to know them. Value your daughter by paying attention to her and her friends, she advises. Let your daughter know how much you appreciate her and her abilities, and support her expectations of her future as a contributing adult in society, be they in the business world or as a mother. From her mother, a daughter can receive support as she continues to develop her female gender characteristics. But that is not all she needs to be a complete adult. She needs to receive support from her father as she, too, separates herself from her mother to become an independent person, one trusting of relationships between men and women. A father need not fear that developing such trust will lead to an innocence that makes life in the real world too dangerous. It will, however, help a girl to grow up with a belief in the basic goodness of people, which will help her to face whatever she encounters as she becomes an adult.

FATHERS AND LEARNING

Research data show that boys reared without a father present often score below average on cognitive tests.[41] Sociologists C.E. Bowerman and G.H. Elder, Jr., found that boys between the ages of thirteen and eighteen who were high scholastic achievers had fathers who were the most powerful individuals in their families. Another researcher reported that high father interaction and a strong, involved father in the family had a significant correlation with the verbal ability of boys, as measured by a standard achievement test.[42] The absence of a father seems to have less effect on a girl's subsequent social and cognitive performance; father interaction seems to encourage higher scores in boys, while mother interaction seems to do the same for girls, three researchers from Northern Illinois University reported.[43] But *both* boys and girls scored higher on achievement tests if they had one full-time parent who spent a considerable amount of time interacting with them, something that is usually possible only when the family includes both a mother and a father. Research conducted at Bowling Green State University and Columbia University compared the American College Entrance Examination scores of 295 students from father-absent homes with those of 769 students from father-present homes. This study concluded that, regardless of the socioeconomic status of the family, the scholastic achievement of students from father-absent homes was "dramatically lower" than that of the students from homes with fathers present.[44]

FATHERS AND PLAY

"Dad, you're fun!" This is a response that many fathers treasure. And since it seems to be a nearly universal statement of bonding between children and their fathers, we can assume that it is no accident that children respond this way to their fathers. Some mothers feel this happens because Dad is usually away all day; by the time he gets home, Mom is exhausted, and Dad, not weighed down with concerns about their daily caretaking, is happy to see his children and ready to play with them. This would seem like a perfectly plausible conclusion. However, research also shows that men are, by nature, the initiators of challenging and rough play. While from their mothers, children are more likely to learn fantasy play and "joint positive play"—in other words, noncompetitive games—fathers encourage their children to stretch their organizational, physical, and mental capabilities.[45] A father is more likely to encourage his child to swim a little faster and beat the clock, to try again to hit a home run, to do better in a board game, or to see who can win at arm wrestling. Within the safety of a play environment, a child can experiment with the type of mind stretching and facing of challenges that he will later face in real life.

Father is usually the baby-tosser and roughhouser in the family. Fathers are so good at play, in fact, that they sometimes feel awkward or even greatly ill at ease with a tiny baby because they don't know what to do with an infant. While a mother may be perfectly content to carry and simply be around her child, many fathers worry about what they should "do with" a baby. They want to play, but an infant is too young to respond in a playful, give-and-take manner.

In his book *On Becoming a Family*, Dr. T. Berry Brazelton notes a fascinating bit of research he has been conducting. With the use of a video camera, and the ability to see the actions, interactions, and reactions of babies and adults in slow motion, he has observed that fathers tend to set up a different pattern of interaction with their babies than mothers do. In particular, he notes, fathers are more playful. They use rhythmic games of tickling or tapping on parts of the baby's body that produce a heightened response from the baby, "exaggerated gestures or expressions [that] seem to say, 'Now let's play.'" As a baby gets older, he will laugh out loud and show every indication of

eagerness to continue the playful interaction with his father. By contrast, when a baby reacts to his mother's presence, "his face will soften, and his legs and arms will begin
to move in a slow, smooth, predictable fashion." A baby's
reaction to his mother is so different that, according to Dr.
Brazelton, "We can block out the screen to watch only a
toe, a finger, a hand, or a foot and predict successfully
whether the baby is in an interaction with his mother or
his father."[46] Even at the tender age of a few weeks, a baby
responds to his parents' different gender characteristics in
like fashion, and they mirror each other. The child needs,
wants, and responds to both the soft, intimate nurturing
of his mother, and the playful, action-oriented encouragement of his father.

This becomes important when one realizes that play is
more than something to enjoy (although it is that also, of
course). Playing is an important means of bonding that
ideally should continue throughout the child-rearing
years. It can serve as a way for a father and child to
communicate and to deepen their relationship. One
woman told me that her father was not easy to communicate with verbally, but that they had always made a point
of playing tennis once a week. The camaraderie that resulted gave them a deep appreciation and love for one
another. Many women lament the general lack of communication skills in men because they themselves are so good
at communicating and thrive on it. But communication is
more than talking. Children seem to understand this instinctively, and bond beautifully in play. And this bonding
brings rewards. "One of the most gratifying of all father
feelings," writes Dr. William Sears, "is sensing that your
child feels comfortable seeking your help."[47] The sense of
comfort and trust established through play—carefully bal-
anced, fearless play—can lay the groundwork for an open
road on which the child can travel to his father for help.

Acceptance through play helps to build self-esteem and create good feelings between fathers and children. According to Karl Zinsmeister, adjunct scholar with the American Enterprise Institute for Public Policy Research, "Babies who have spent a great deal of time with their fathers are more sociable, vocalize more, show a greater love of play and seem more eager to be picked up."[48]

In addition to being an important means of bonding between fathers and children, play can also enhance intellectual development. Many of us are under the impression that as long as children have toys to play with, they should be happy playing by themselves. Millions of dollars are spent each year on toys and play equipment, to entertain children or to make daycare centers "fun to be in." While they may satisfy a child's curiosity for a while, most of these toys do not invite extensive manipulation, exploration, or inventive or imaginative activity on the part of the child. They are no substitute for human interaction, in which a child can experience encouragement, joint imagination and exploration, and exposure to new ideas. Two minds working together create, in effect, a third mind, which comes about as ideas build on one another. Because of his inherent male orientation toward play and the seeking of challenges, a father is usually uniquely well suited to offer his child this type of interaction. We have all heard the criticism that television stifles imagination. Some people blame the schools for not doing more to exercise the minds of students through imagination-expansion games. But it seems to me that the low level of interaction between many children and fathers, who are especially good at play that helps to stimulate problem-solving and to challenge skills and ideas, may also be to blame for the lack of development of imagination and wasted intellectual resources among so many of today's children.

Through play, children can learn to grow toward independence and expand their horizons, and fathers seem to be especially good at helping this to happen. But all of this takes time. Parents have to choose to take time to make it happen—time away from television, hobbies, and work. It doesn't happen on its own. It requires that we take time away from self-fulfillment and devote it instead to our children's development. Being a parent requires more than a when-it-is-convenient, how-about-next-week, if-I-am-in-the-mood, if-I-have-time kind of scheduling. Human interaction takes time.

FATHERS, MOTHERS, AND CHILDREN

Children can be reared by a single parent, whether opposite- or same-sex, and still do well. Children can be reared in daycare centers, by aunts, or in foster homes. Children are adaptable and can survive in a variety of environments. Often, they have to. But ideally, when all is said and done, the most favorable environment for a child includes both mother and father, because each offers a unique perspective on life. Sounds idealistic? Most children would not say so. Instinctively, they know they have a need for both.

It is the difference between men and women, their different gender characteristics, that provides a unique and total growing-up experience for the child. The greatest challenge in child rearing is to achieve an appropriate balance between the two and to figure out when a child needs more of one than the other. This is a balancing act that prescriptions or formulas cannot address. Child rearing therefore will always be a challenge. Parents will always have to try to attain the best combination of the input of both mother and father, female and male. To do this, they must recognize and accept each partner's unique role in the child-rearing process.

In response to the increasing splintering of the family in the last few decades, many books have been written supporting the necessity of mother-child interaction. Indeed, few would argue that mothers are not important. But even though equally convincing evidence is available to support the importance of fathers in families, this has never received as much attention or been as widely accepted as important. We owe it to our children to seek to appreciate the importance of the father in a child's life, to bring his role into perspective, and to bring to light the benefits his involvement can offer children. If mother is the touchstone as the *nurturer* in the family, father is the touchstone as the *encourager*.

"There is, of course, no absolutely right or wrong way
of helping even one child to grow up.
There are merely *facts* which indicate that perhaps
one way of child care may be more desirable
than another way of child care."

Niles Newton, Ph.D. (1957)

"Most of us raise youngsters on the basis of
our own needs rather than theirs.
An uncomfortable thought, but true."

Dorothy Corkille Briggs (1975)

"It's clear that most American children suffer
too much mother and too little father."

Gloria Steinem

"Infants are fully capable of learning to manipulate
their parents. . . . Thus, a healthy baby can keep his
mother hopping around his nursery twelve hours
a day (or night) by simply forcing air past
his sandpaper larynx."

James C. Dobson, Ph.D. (1984)

". . . the best results in working with children of any
age come when we respect the child's
maturity level and his own time table."

Louise Bates Ames, Ph.D. (1987)

Conclusion

As we have seen, there is a difference between the way in which men and women approach child rearing. Both approaches are needed, because they complement each other. Many mothers experience great conflict, however, because they are trying to raise their children according to a male approach, while ignoring their own feelings. This does not work, and it is not good for the children.

I know that many of the examples of gender characteristics can be argued against—"But I don't fit that at all!" or, "My husband is just the opposite." But the point of this book has been to create an awareness of the gender differences between the generic man and the generic woman in their approach to child rearing, *not* to imply that all women (or all men) are alike. Each individual, after all, possesses a unique combination of characteristics. But with all of the things men and women have in common—and with all of the differences between individual men and women—there are nevertheless basic tendencies common to each gender, and these gender characteristics cut across all lines of culture, environment, and time.

Historically and globally, women have been—and still are today—the primary caretakers of young children. In many traditional cultures, a male child stays with his mother until he reaches a certain age, at which time he is also taken into the men's world to continue maturing toward manhood. Girls, meanwhile, remain closer to their mothers and the female world, as they develop toward womanhood. From ancient Egyptian sculpture to pre-Columbian clay figures, from Indian tapestries to the paintings of Picasso, women are portrayed as the nurturers. "Throughout history, poets and painters, novelists and dramatists looked to the relationship of mother and child as an inspiration for some of their greatest works," writes Gail Harvey in *A Mother Is Love.*[1]

I am convinced that the overwhelming majority of male doctors and experts genuinely believe that the child-rearing advice they give mothers is in the best interests of children, families, and society. These men stepped into the role of adviser when, in the late 1800s and early 1900s, new mothers were left stranded, away from family and a close-knit society, faced with new technologies, new discoveries, and a revolutionary new way of life. A tremendous new wave washed over the Western world, bearing the label "new and improved." Men became enamored of scientific discoveries. They did not stop with engines and medicine and chemicals, but tested new ideas on human behavior as well. The behaviorist Dr. John Watson, once a popular and frequent contributor to *Harper's, McCall's,* and *Cosmopolitan* magazines, wrote in 1928, "No one knows enough to raise a child. The world would be considerably better off if we were to stop having children for 20 years (except those reared for experimental purposes) and were then to start again with enough facts to do the job with some degree of skill and accuracy. Parenthood, instead of being an instinctive art, is a science, the details of which must be worked out by patient laboratory methods."[2] The prevailing attitude came to be (as it remains today) that if we trained parents, society would be better off. Books on child rearing became a "must-have" for every young mother. In Sweden, it was even suggested that no woman should be allowed to have a child until she attended a course in child rearing (although no mention was made of who exactly would be qualified to teach it).[3]

It was the early 1900s, the dawn of a new century, and women listened. They wanted to join the new world. Children and child rearing became a focus of intense attention. The National Congress of Mothers was formed; so were the PTA, the International Kindergarten Union, and university-based child study centers and laboratories. A new slogan led the research: "The future of the race marches forward on the feet of little children."[4] But in their awe and enthusiasm for all that was new, women relinquished their own knowledge and expertise, and followed the instructions of the prominent researchers of the time—men. These men did not actually know very much about rearing little children, although they did the best they could. And some of their work probably did help in some ways, such as improving hygiene practices, and improving working conditions for children. But they did not limit themselves to situations that needed improvement. Instead, they took over the entire field of parenting, from pregnancy and childbirth to breast-feeding and child rearing, from the abnormal cases to the normal. Based on their research and observations—all seen and experienced through the filter of their masculine perspective—they advised mothers on how to care for their children. They wrote books that were based on their own gender-specific thinking, and urged others to strive for the things they most valued in themselves: independence, autonomy, and self-reliance. This male value system was then impressed on women and, in turn, on children, from infancy on. It made sense to men. It brought tears and frustration to mothers and babies.

From the moment of birth, the child begins to grow toward the father. For the first few months the growing is almost imperceptible, though. The newborn child is by nature completely dependent and needs total immersion in intimacy and connectedness, things her mother is uniquely suited to provide. Over time, as the child grows, she slowly begins to wean herself from her mother and comes to need the encouragement and guidance of her father to develop into an independent person in her own right. This is true for both boys and girls, although girls ultimately remain in the female world with their mothers as they develop their femininity. A boy child, however, as he weans himself from his mother, absolutely must have someone else—a man—ready to encourage and groom his developing masculinity in order to develop a healthy sense of male identity.

Children need both a mother and a father during their growing years. They need nurturing from their mother and encouragement from their father. There is an increasing amount of evidence to support the claim that children of both sexes need the benefits of the gender characteristics of both parents.

Child rearing is a delicate balancing act in which parents are forever trying to figure out the best approach to use. I believe that understanding the implications of each parent's gender-specific approach will help to make parenting easier, as well as more fair to children. Mothers would do well to be sensitive to what it means for men in our culture to become more aware of their wives' feelings. This is not easy for men, because they receive very little support from society for doing so. After all, many child-rearing books tell them that their feelings are the right ones.

For their part, fathers need to understand why their wives feel and respond the way they do, and to realize that their nurturing feelings are not expressions of defiance (of their husbands or of the male experts) but of maternal emotions. It is okay for men and women to have different approaches; in fact, it is natural. It does *not* mean that one must be right and the other wrong.

In the past hundred years or so, women's emotions and values have more or less been ignored. The male perspective has been taken as the norm, and few people bothered to question whether women saw the world the same way. Fathers, meanwhile, were to a large extent left out of the child-rearing picture altogether. Their role is still not much honored or respected by our society. Little is recognized, for instance, of their vital importance as role models for the development of healthy masculinity in their sons. The father's role as supporter and teacher, and his importance in play and learning, have all been belittled, scoffed at, or ignored.

One husband and father said to me, "Your ideas really irritate me, in a way, because I am now no longer the authority in my family, the one who is always right. Now I have to remember how my wife feels, and that bothers me." When I chuckled, he said, "Hey, don't laugh. I am dead serious. If I have to understand that women have these feelings and that they are justified, then women have to understand that the father's argument is good, too. Children *should* experience life and face the consequences of their actions, as long as they are not life threatening. Just as we can't be autocratic fathers, we can't have dominating mothers, either, who smother their kids with protectiveness, who constantly hover over them and restrain them within *her* comfort limits." And he's right. But the kind of characteristically female nurturing I have been describing does not mean tugging and restraining and smothering with protection. Nor does male encouragement mean pushing a child beyond her limits. There is a wide middle ground here. I realize it is difficult for some men to see that advocating respect for women's approach to child rearing does not mean undermining their own importance, and men need to feel important, loved, and respected. But if both men and women could consciously decide not to be judgmental but instead to seek to better understand each other's approach, as well as the needs of their children, we would all be better off. We wouldn't need to feel so defensive about our authority, our intentions, our worth as human beings, or our abilities as mothers and fathers. When we can understand where another person is coming from, we can better understand, evaluate, and talk about where we ourselves are coming from, and attempt to work together for a win-win outcome.

When a father is involved in raising his child, he is more tuned in to the child's need for connectedness and more aware of the child's level of readiness to expand her horizons. Likewise, when a mother is intimately connected with her child she is more aware of the child's needs and of her readiness to handle new experiences and to benefit from her father's urging to face challenges. Through understanding, we can embrace both our own and our partners' points of view, not only to meet the needs of our children, but to strengthen and embrace the purpose of the family as a whole.

Children do best when their parents are available but too busy to hover around very much. This gives children the combination of security and freedom they need to grow, to explore, to try new adventures, and even to get hurt and learn to soothe themselves. If a child needs comforting, she will seek it. Usually a quick observation will reveal how serious her hurt is and whether it requires coming to her aid. When my children hurt themselves and began to cry, or rushed to the bathroom to be sick, I always asked them, "Do you need my help?" Since I am a firm believer in children's sense about themselves, I trusted their answers. The secret to knowing how much to nurture or to encourage is to rely on the child's input. If you do this from birth on, you set up a very straightforward, honest, and reliable system that takes much of the guesswork out of parenting. The child knows she will receive help or comfort when she needs it; the parents know that she will let them know when she needs them. The child will also usually let it be known which parent she wants or needs at that particular moment. Trust your child. Children are often much wiser than we give them credit for.

Because we all, parents and children alike, have different inherent physiological and psychological systems, and face internal and external situations that change constantly, and because every human relationship is unique, I cannot conclude this book with ten simple steps for reducing child-rearing conflicts and having a happier family life. If life were only that simple! When is a tree limb *too* high? When is a frustration *too* long? When is nurturing *too* much? All too often, the answer is, "That depends. . ." (a typically female answer, of course). We are so accustomed to being able to look up the right answer for any problem in a book, and so little trained to take suggestions and input and make intelligent decisions for our own situation. We've all read the books that promise "step-by-step solutions," "easy-to-follow procedures," "one-minute answers," and so on, as if life were as easy to solve as one, two, three. "Today," writes Wendy Kaminer in *I'm Dysfunctional, You're Dysfunctional*, "even critical books about ideas are expected to be prescriptive, to conclude with simple step-by-step solutions. . ."[5] This mindset has robbed us of a feeling of empowerment to take new insights and knowledge and use them on our own. But solutions offered by others are not nearly as profound or useful as the solutions people come up with for themselves, as a result of contemplating thought-provoking information that intrigues them. We would do well to take a step back from our own positions and ask each other, "How would you solve that problem? What do you think is the answer?" We might all learn a great deal if we started actively listening more. Of course, like any worthwhile endeavor, this too takes time.

In this book I have offered the reader some of my own ideas and answers, based on my twenty-four years of mothering and fifty-plus years as a woman. I hope they will lead to such thoughts as: Based on the information in this book, do I understand my spouse better? Will this insight require making adjustments? If so, what will I do differently?

Finally, a brief word about guilt. Guilt is only good when it results in change. Not infrequently, parents approach me with great concern about the way they have handled their children and their own frustrations in the child-rearing process in the past. But the past is gone. We have to look toward the future. We should be excited about being able to change today for the benefit of tomorrow. Guilt can be good if it forces us to reassess and reconsider our actions. But no one will ever be perfect, or always right. We are forever learning, and most of us are doing the best we can. Be gentle with yourself, and with others. All of life is a learning experience, and it can be beautiful.

If you are a parent, focus on your child. Walt Whitman wrote:

> There was a child went forth every day;
> And the first object he looked upon, that object he became;
> And that object became part of him for the day, or a certain
>   part of the day, or for many years, or stretching cycles of
>   years.[6]

Children learn what they live. A child needs both a mother and a father; her mother's approach and her father's approach. Men and women, fathers and mothers, have always had different approaches to child rearing. But unlike people in the past, we find ourselves living in a world where the majority of child-rearing advice comes from men, while it is women who are the primary caretakers of young children. So it is vitally important that we come to understand these differences, and then learn to accept and celebrate them, for the good of our children.

Notes

Chapter One
The Mother Parenting versus Father Parenting Conflict

1. Marshall H. Klaus and John H. Kennell, *Maternal-Infant Bonding* (St. Louis: C.V. Mosby Company, 1976), ix.
2. Deborah Tannen, *You Just Don't Understand: Women and Men in Conversation* (New York: William Morrow and Company, 1990), 122.
3. Robert May, *Sex and Fantasy* (New York: W.W. Norton and Company, 1980), xi.
4. "Where Are Women and Men Today? Robert Bly and Deborah Tannen in Conversation," *New Age Journal*, February 1992, 75.
5. Alice Gerard, *Please Breast-Feed Your Baby* (New York: New American Library, 1970), 103.
6. A. Towle, *Fathers* (New York: Simon and Schuster, 1986), 231.

Chapter Two
Understanding Basic Gender Differences

1. Robert May, *Sex and Fantasy* (New York: W.W. Norton and Company, 1980), 1.
2. Niles Newton, *Newton on Birth and Women* (Seattle, WA: Birth and Life Bookstore, 1990), 256.
3. Anafasia Toufexis, "Coming From a Different Place," *Time*, Special Women's Issue (Fall 1990), 64.
4. Cris Evatt, *He and She* (Berkeley, CA: Conari Press, 1992), 14.
5. Ibid.
6. "Where Are Women and Men Today? Robert Bly and Deborah Tannen in Conversation," *New Age Journal*, February 1992, 92.

7. Robert May, *Sex and Fantasy* (New York: W.W. Norton and Company, 1980), 77.
8. Ibid., 97.
9. Carol Gilligan, *In a Different Voice* (Cambridge, MA: Harvard University Press, 1982), 7.
10. Anafasia Toufexis, "Coming From a Different Place," *Time*, Special Women's Issue (Fall 1990), 65.
11. Cris Evatt, *He and She* (Berkeley, CA: Conari Press, 1992), 19.
12. Deborah Tannen, *You Just Don't Understand: Women and Men in Conversation* (New York: William Morrow and Company, 1990), 43.
13. Ibid., 44.
14. Mary Field Belenky et al., *Women's Ways of Knowing* (New York: Basic Books, 1986), 18.
15. Rita Kramer, *In Defense of the Family* (New York: Basic Books, 1983), 66.
16. Anne Moir and David Jessel, *Brain Sex* (New York: Lyle Stewart, 1991), 5.
17. Robert May, *Sex and Fantasy* (New York: W.W. Norton and Company, 1980), 98.
18. Carol Gilligan, *In a Different Voice* (Cambridge, MA: Harvard University Press, 1982), 8.
19. Deborah Tannen, *You Just Don't Understand: Women and Men in Conversation* (New York: William Morrow and Company, 1990), 81.
20. Ibid., 108.
21. Cris Evatt, *He and She* (Berkeley, CA: Conari Press, 1992), 42.
22. Thomas Verny and Pamela Weintraub, *Nurturing the Unborn Child* (New York: Dell Publishing, 1991).
23. John A. Sanford and George Lough, *What Men Are Like* (New York: Paulist Press, 1988), 20.
24. Cris Evatt, *He and She* (Berkeley, CA: Conari Press, 1992), 38.
25. Carol Gilligan, *In a Different Voice* (Cambridge, MA: Harvard University Press, 1982), 14.

Chapter Three
Understanding Basic Parenting Differences

1. Barton D. Schmitt, *Your Child's Health* (New York: Bantam Books, 1987), 107.
2. Miriam Lewin, ed., *In the Shadow of the Past: Psychology Portrays the Sexes* (New York: Columbia University Press, 1984), 150.
3. *The American Heritage Dictionary of the English Language*, Third Edition (Boston: Houghton Mifflin Company, 1992), 2112.

4. Cris Evatt, *He and She* (Berkeley, CA: Conari Press, 1992), 16.
5. Benjamin Spock, *Baby and Child Care* (New York: Pocket Books, 1971), 192.
6. Martin Richards, ed., *The Integration of a Child Into a Social World* (London: Cambridge University Press, 1974), 121.
7. Ibid., 12.
8. Niles Newton, *Newton on Birth and Women* (Seattle, WA: Birth and Life Bookstore, 1990), 125.
9. Lee Salk, *What Every Child Would Like His Parents to Know* (New York: David McKay Company, 1972), 35.
10. Virginia F. Pomeranz, *The First Five Years* (New York: St. Martin's Press, 1984), 17.
11. *The Womanly Art of Breastfeeding*. (Franklin Park, IL: La Leche League International, 1991), 170.
12. Selma Fraiberg, *Every Child's Birthright* (New York: Basic Books, 1977), 81.
13. James McKenna, "Researching the Sudden Infant Death Syndrome (SIDS): The Role of Ideology in the Biomedical Sciences," monograph series of the New Liberal Arts Program, Research Foundation of the State University of New York at Stony Brook (1991), 6.
14. James J. McKenna, "SIDS Research," *Mothering*, No. 65 (Winter 1992), 48.
15. James McKenna, "Researching the Sudden Infant Death Syndrome (SIDS): The Role of Ideology in the Biomedical Sciences," monograph series of the New Liberal Arts Program, Research Foundation of the State University of New York at Stony Brook (1991).
16. Selma Fraiberg, *Every Child's Birthright* (New York: Basic Books, 1977), 61.
17. *Quotes and Comments on Mother/Baby Separation* (Franklin Park, IL: La Leche League International.
18. David Elkind, *The Hurried Child* (Reading, MA: Addison-Wesley Publishing Company, 1981).
19. Anne Moir and David Jessel, *Brain Sex* (New York: Lyle Stewart, 1991), 148.
20. David Elkind, *The Hurried Child* (Reading, MA: Addison-Wesley Publishing Company, 1981), xii.
21. Selma Fraiberg, *Every Child's Birthright* (New York: Basic Books, 1977), 80.
22. James McKenna, "Researching the Sudden Infant Death Syndrome (SIDS)," monograph series of the New Liberal Arts Program, Research Foundation of the State University of New York at Stony Brook (1991), 28.

Chapter Four
Reading the Experts

1. Alice Judson Ryerson, "Medical Advice on Childrearing 1550-1990," *Harvard Educational Review* 31:302 (1961), 220.
2. Ibid, 216.
3. Sirgay Sanger and John Kelly, *You and Your Baby's First Year* (New York: Bantam Books, 1987), 20.
4. Stanley Greenspan, *First Feelings* (New York: Viking Penguin, Inc., 1985), 16.
5. Heidi L. Brennan, brochure introducing *Discovering Motherhood*, ed. Heidi L. Brennan (Vienna, VA: Mothers at Home, 1991).
6. Penelope Leach, *Your Baby and Child From Birth to Age Five* (New York: Alfred A. Knopf, Inc., 1989), 8.
7. Robin Lakoff, *Talking Power* (New York: Basic Books, 1990).
8. Eileen Shiff, *Experts Advise Parents* (New York: Bantam, Doubleday, Dell Publishing Group, 1987), xxi.
9. Barton D. Schmitt, *Your Child's Health* (New York: Bantam Books, 1987), 146.
10. Alvin Eden, *Positive Parenting* (New York: New American Library, Inc., 1980), 41.
11. Robin Goldstein, *Everyday Parenting* (Rockville, MD: AriAnna Press, 1987), 72.
12. Barton D. Schmitt, *Your Child's Health* (New York: Bantam Books, 1987), 207.
13. Robin Goldstein, *Everyday Parenting* (Rockville, MD: AriAnna Press, 1987), 106.
14. Richard Ferber, *Experts Advise Parents*, ed. Eileen Shiff (New York: Bantam, Doubleday, Dell Publishing Group, 1987), 83.
15. Cris Evatt, *He and She* (Berkeley, CA: Conari Press, 1992), 80.
16. Ibid., 30.
17. Richard Ferber, *Experts Advise Parents*, ed. Eileen Shiff (New York: Bantam, Doubleday, Dell Publishing Group, 1987), 68.
18. Ibid., 71.
19. Sheila Kitzinger, *Women As Mothers* (New York: First Vintage Books, September 1980), 5.
20. Eda LeShan *When Your Child Drives You Crazy* (New York: St. Martin's Paperbacks, 1985), 38.
21. T. Berry Brazelton, *To Listen to a Child.* (Reading, MA: Merloyd Lawrence Inc., 1984), 55.
22. Ibid., 120.
23. Benjamin Spock, *Baby and Child Care* (New York: Pocket Books, 1971), 26.

24. Deborah Tannen, *You Just Don't Understand: Women and Men in Conversation* (New York: William Morrow and Company, 1990), 117.

25. Irene M. Josselyn, *Psychological Development of Children* (New York: Family Service Association of America, 1967), 19.

26. Diana Bert et al., *After Having a Baby* (New York: Dell Publishing, 1988), 239.

27. Robin Goldstein, *Everyday Parenting* (Rockville, MD: AriAnna Press, 1987), 40.

Chapter Five
The Importance of the Nurturing Mother

1. John Whiting, "Environmental Constraints on Infant Care Practices," *Handbook of Cross-Cultural Human Development,* ed. Robert Monroe, Ruth Monroe, and Beatrice Whiting (New York: Garland STPN Press, 1981), 155.

2. John M. Whiting, "22 Effects of Climate on Certain Cultural Practices," *Explorations in Cultural Anthropology,* ed. W.H. Goodenough (New York: McGraw-Hill, 1964), 416–544.

3. Susan B. Tobey, *Art of Motherhood* (New York: Abbeville Press Publishers, 1991), 99.

4. Selma Fraiberg, "How a Baby Learns to Love," *Redbook,* May 1971, 76.

5. Harriet E. Gross, "Considering 'A Biosocial Perspective on Parenting,'" *Signs: Journal of Women on Culture and Society,* Vol. 4 No. 4 (University of Chicago, 1979).

6. Susan B. Tobey, *Art of Motherhood* (New York: Abbeville Press Publishers, 1991), 111.

7. Institute for American Values, *Family Affairs,* Vol. 4 No. 1/2 (Winter/Spring 1991), 2.

8. Peter Cook, "Childrearing, Culture and Mental Health," *Medical Journal of Australia,* Special Supplement (August 12, 1978), 3.

9. Ibid., 8.

10. Mihaly Csikszentmihalyi, *Flow: The Psychology of Optimal Experience* (New York: HarperCollins, 1990), 168.

11. Ibid., 164.

12. Deborah Jackson, *Three in a Bed* (New York: Avon Books, 1989).

13. "Unite and Conquer," *Newsweek,* 5 February 1990, 5.

14. *The First Three Years* (Cincinnati, OH: Foundation for the Family, 1988).

15. Ibid.

16. Ibid.

17. Ashley Montagu, *Touching* (New York: Columbia University Press, 1971), 28.
18. Ibid., 45.
19. Susan Flagler Virden, "The Relationship Between Infant Feeding Method and Maternal Role Adjustment," *Journal of Nurse Midwifery*, Vol. 33 No. 1 (January 1988), 34.
20. Jan Riordan and Kathleen G. Auerbach, *Breastfeeding and Human Lactation* (Boston: Jones and Bartlett, 1993), 105.
21. *The First Three Years* (Cincinnati, OH: Foundation for the Family, 1988).
22. Sheila Kippley, *Breastfeeding and Natural Child Spacing* (Cincinnati: Couple to Couple League, 1974).
23. James J. McKenna, "SIDS Research," *Mothering*, No. 65 (Winter 1992), 48.
24. Ibid.
25. Ibid., 50.
26. Niles Newton, *Newton on Birth and Women* (Seattle, WA: Birth and Life Bookstore, 1990), 118.
27. Marshall H. Klaus and John H. Kennell, *Maternal-Infant Bonding*. (St. Louis: C.V. Mosby Company, 1976), 59–68.
28. Peter S. Cook "Childrearing, Culture and Mental Health," *The Medical Journal of Australia*, Special Supplement (August 12, 1978), 5.
29. Susan Flagler Virden, "The Relationship Between Infant Feeding Method and Maternal Role Adjustment," *Journal of Nurse Midwifery*, Vol. 33 No. 1 (January 1988), 34.
30. Ner Littner, *Custody and Visitation Arrangements* (Franklin Park, IL: La Leche League International).
31. Peter Cook, "Childrearing, Culture and Mental Health," *Medical Journal of Australia*, Special Supplement (August 12, 1978), 6.
32. Elizabeth Wrigley, and Sally Hutchinson, "Long-Term Breastfeeding: The Secret Bond," *Journal of Nurse-Midwifery*, Vol. 35 No. 1 (January/February 1990), 35.
33. Joseph C. Pearce, *Magical Child Matures* (New York: E.P. Dutton, Inc., 1985), 27.
34. Cris Evatt, *He and She* (Berkeley, CA: Conari Press, 1992), 130.
35. Ibid., 14.
36. Institute for American Values, *Family Affairs*, Vol. 4 No. 1/2 (Winter/Spring 1991), 12.
37. Anne Moir and David Jessel, *Brain Sex* (New York: Lyle Stewart, 1991).
38. *Stephen Hawking's A Brief History of Time: A Reader's Companion,*

ed. S. Hawking, prepared by Gene Stone (New York: Bantam Books, 1992), 61.

39. Elizabeth Barrett Browning, *Aurora Leigh*, in *The Complete Poetical Works of Mrs. Browning*, Cambridge Edition (Boston: Houghton Mifflin Company, 1900), 255.

40. Alice Rossi, "A Biosocial Perspective on Parenting," *Daedalus*, Spring 1977, 25.

41. Huston Smith, *The Religions of Man* (New York: Harper and Row, 1991), 482.

42. Peter S. Cook "Childrearing, Culture and Mental Health," *The Medical Journal of Australia*, Special Supplement (August 12, 1978), 3.

43. T. Berry Brazelton, *On Becoming a Family* (New York: Dell Publishing, 1992), 184.

Chapter Six
The Importance of the Encouraging Father

1. Institute for American Values, *Family Affairs*, Vol. 4 No. 1/2 (Winter/Spring 1991), 1.

2. Margaret Mead, *Letters From the Field: 1925-1975* (New York: Harper and Row, 1977), quoted in Ken Heyman, *The World's Family* (New York: Putnam Publishing Group, 1983), 8.

3. Jean Liedloff, *The Continuum Concept* (Reading, MA: Addison-Wesley Publishing Group, 1985), 82.

4. Sally Quinn, "The Feminist Betrayal," *Reader's Digest*, June 1992, 84.

5. Mona Charen, column in the *Savannah (Georgia) News*, 16 February 1992.

6. Robert Bly, *Iron John* (New York: Vintage Books, 1992), 22.

7. David Blankenhorn, *The Good Family Man* (New York: Institute for American Values, November 1991).

8. Christopher Hallowell, *Father to the Man* (New York: William Morrow and Company, 1987), 14.

9. Sheila Kitzinger, *Women As Mothers* (New York: First Vintage Books, September 1980), 76.

10. Miriam Lewin, ed., *In the Shadow of the Past: Psychology Portrays the Sexes* (New York: Columbia University Press, 1984), 1.

11. Jane Swigart, *The Myth of the Bad Mother* (New York: Doubleday, 1991), 115.

12. Wade Macky, "Parameters of the Adult-Male Child," *Ethology and Sociobiology*, 1:59-76 1979 (Elsevier North Holland Inc., 1979), 60.

13. Ibid., 22–32, 73.
14. Sirgay Sanger and John Kelly, *You and Your Baby's First Year* (New York: Bantam Books, 1987), 222.
15. Robert Bly, *Iron John* (New York: Vintage Books, 1992), 18.
16. Wade Macky, "Parameters of the Adult-Male Child," *Ethology and Sociobiology*, 1:59-76 1979 (Elsevier North Holland Inc., 1979), 59.
17. William Sears, *Creative Parenting* (New York, Dodd, Mead & Company, 1987), 12.
18. John Gray, *Men, Women and Relationships* (Hillsboro, OR: Beyond Words Publications, 1990), quoted in Cris Evatt, *He and She* (Berkeley, CA: Conari Press, 1992), 14.
19. Scott Coltrane, "Father-Child Relationships and the Status of Women: A Cross-Cultural Study," *American Journal of Sociology*, Vol. 93 No. 5 (March 1988), 1060–1095.
20. William Sears, *Creative Parenting* (New York, Dodd, Mead & Company, 1987), 90.
21. M. Scott Peck, *The Road Less Traveled* (New York: Simon and Schuster, 1978), 15.
22. Mona Charen, column in the *Savannah (Georgia) News*, 16 February 1992.
23. Institute for American Values, *Family Affairs*, Vol. 4 No. 1/2 (Winter/Spring 1991), 13.
24. *Quotes and Comments on Mother/Baby Separation* (Franklin Park, IL: La Leche League International).
25. R.E. Emery, E.M. Hetherington, and L.F. Dilalla, "Divorce, Children and Social Policy," *Child Development Research and Social Policy*, Volume 1, ed. Harold W. Stevenson and Alberta E. Siegel (Chicago: University of Chicago Press, 1984), 209.
26. Ibid.
27. William Sears, *Becoming a Father* (Franklin Park, IL: La Leche League International, 1986), 178.
28. Robert Bly, *Iron John* (New York: Vintage Books, 1992), 94.
29. Howard Sivertson, "A Family Tradition," *Once Upon an Isle* (Mount Horeb, WI: Wisconsin Folk Museum, 1992), 81.
30. David Blankenhorn, *The Good Family Man* (New York: Institute for American Values, November 1991), 16.
31. Robert Bly, *Iron John* (New York: Vintage Books, 1992), 25.
32. Rita Kramer, *In Defense of the Family* (New York: Basic Books, 1983), 185.
33. David Blankenhorn, *The Good Family Man* (New York: Institute for American Values, November 1991), 16.
34. David Blankenhorn, quoted in Murray Dubin, "Linking Social

Ills and Absent Fathers," *The Philadelphia Inquirer*, 10 January 1992.

35. Thomas Sowell, "The Big Lie," *Forbes*, 23 December 1991.
36. Institute for American Values, *The Family in America*, Vol. 2 No. 8 (August 1988), 5.
37. Bernard Weiner, "Initiating Our Teenage Sons," *Mothering*, No. 67 (Summer 1993), 91.
38. Phyllis Theroux, *Night Lights* (New York: Viking Penguin, 1987), 35.
39. Rita Kramer, *In Defense of the Family* (New York: Basic Books, 1983), 68.
40. Irwin Garfinkel and Sara S. McLanahan, *Single Mothers and Their Children: A New American Dilemma* (Washington, DC: Urban Institute Press, 1986), 66.
41. Samuel Osherson, *Finding Our Fathers* (New York: Fawcett Columbine, 1986), 223.
42. Institute for American Values, *The Family in America*, Vol. 2 No. 8 (August 1988), 2.
43. Ibid.
44. Ibid., 4.
45. Ibid., 2.
46. T. Berry Brazelton, *On Becoming a Family* (New York: Dell Publishing, 1992), 143.
47. William Sears, *Becoming a Father* (Franklin Park, IL: La Leche League International, 1986), 88.
48. Uhlenbuth, Karen, "Life Without Father," *Kansas City Star*, 23 February 1992.

Conclusion

1. Gail Harvey, ed., *A Mother Is Love* (New York: Gramercy Books, 1992).
2. Miriam Lewin, ed., *In the Shadow of the Past: Psychology Portrays the Sexes* (New York: Columbia University Press, 1984), 139.
3. Sheila Kitzinger, *Women As Mothers* (New York: First Vintage Books, September 1980), 6.
4. Miriam Lewin, ed., *In the Shadow of the Past: Psychology Portrays the Sexes* (New York: Columbia University Press, 1984), 133.
5. Wendy Kaminer, *I'm Dysfunctional, You're Dysfunctional* (New York: Addison-Wesley Publishing Company, 1992), 8.
6. Walt Whitman, *Leaves of Grass* (New York: Viking Press, 1945), 168.

Bibliography

Ames, Louise Bates. *Questions Parents Ask*. New York: Bantam, Doubleday, Dell Publishing Group, Inc., 1988.

Ames, Louise Bates, and Frances Ilg. *The Gesell Institute's Child Behavior*. New York: Dell Publishing Company, 1955.

Aries, P. *Centuries of Childhood: A Social History of Family Life*. New York: Random House, 1962.

Belenky, Mary Field, Blythe McVicker Clinchy, Nancy Rule Goldberger, and Jill Mattuck Tarule. *Women's Ways of Knowing*. New York: Basic Books, 1986.

Bert, Diana, Katherine Dusay, Susan Keel, Mary Oei, and Jan Yanehiro. *After Having a Baby*. New York: Dell Publishing, 1988.

Bingham, Sam. "Where Animals Save the Land." *World Monitor*, September 1990.

Blankenhorn, David. *The Good Family Man*. New York: Institute for American Values, November 1991.

Bly, Robert. *Iron John*. New York: Vintage Books, 1992.

Brazelton, T. Berry. "What Parents Told Me About Handling Children's Sleep Problems." *Redbook*, October 1978.

Brazelton, T. Berry. *On Becoming a Family*. New York: Dell Publishing, 1992.

Brazelton, T. Berry. *To Listen to a Child*. Reading, MA: Merloyd Lawrence Inc., 1984.

Brennan, Heidi L., ed. *Discovering Motherhood*. Vienna, VA: Mothers at Home, 1991.

Briggs, Dorothy Corkille. *Your Child's Self-Esteem*. Garden City, NY: Dolphin Books, 1975.

Browning, Elizabeth Barrett. *The Complete Poetical Works of Mrs. Browning*, Cambridge Edition. Boston: Houghton Mifflin Company, 1900.

Bumgarner, Norma Jane. *Mothering Your Nursing Toddler*. Franklin Park, IL: La Leche League International, 1982.

Campbell, Joseph. *The Power of Myth*. New York: Doubleday, 1988.

Caplan, Frank, and Theresa Caplan. *The Power of Play*. Garden City, NY: Doubleday, 1973.

Clarke, Jean Illsley. *Self-Esteem, A Family Affair*. Minneapolis: Winston Press, Inc., 1978.

Cohn, Anna R., and Lucinda A. Leach, eds. *Generations*. New York: Pantheon Books, 1987.

Colijn, Helen. *Of Dutch Ways*. Minneapolis, MN: Dillon Press, Inc., 1980.

Coltrane, Scott. "Father-Child Relationships and the Status of Women: A Cross-Cultural Study." *American Journal of Sociology*, Vol. 93 No. 5, March 1988.

Cook, Peter S. "Childrearing, Culture and Mental Health." *The Medical Journal of Australia*, Special Supplement, August 12, 1978.

Csikszentmihalyi, Mihaly. *Flow: The Psychology of Optimal Experience*. New York: HarperCollins, 1990.

Cuthbertson, Joanne, and Susie Schevill. *Helping Your Child Sleep Through the Night*. New York: Doubleday, 1985.

Densmore, Frances. *Chippewa Customs*. St. Paul, MN: Minnesota Historical Society Press, 1979.

Dyer, Wayne W. *How to Raise Happy Kids*. New York: Avon Books, 1985.

Eden, Alvin. *Positive Parenting*. New York: New American Library, Inc., 1980.

Elkind, David. *The Hurried Child*. Reading, MA: Addison-Wesley Publishing Company, 1981.

Emery, R.E., E.M. Hetherington, and L.F. Dilalla. "Divorce, Children, and Social Policy." *Child Development Research and Social Policy*, Volume 1, ed. Harold W. Stevenson and Alberta E. Siegel. Chicago: University of Chicago Press, 1984.

Encyclopedia of Associations, 20th Edition, Vol. 1. Detroit, MI: Gale Research Company, 1986.

Evatt, Cris. *He and She*. Berkeley, CA: Conari Press, 1992.

Fausto-Sterling, Anne. *Myths of Gender*. New York: Basic Books, 1985.

The First Three Years. Cincinnati, OH: Foundation for the Family, 1988.

Fraiberg, Selma. *Every Child's Birthright*. New York: Basic Books, 1977.

Fraiberg, Selma. "How a Baby Learns to Love." *Redbook*, May 1971.

Garfinkel, Irwin, and Sara S. McLanahan. *Single Mothers and Their Children: A New American Dilemma*. Washington, DC: Urban Institute Press, 1986.

Gerard, Alice. *Please Breast-Feed Your Baby*. New York: New American Library, 1970.

Gibbs, Nancy. "The Dreams of Youth." *Time*, Special Women's Issue, Fall 1990.

Gilligan, Carol. *In a Different Voice*. Cambridge, MA: Harvard University Press, 1982.

Goldstein, Robin. *Everyday Parenting*. Rockville, MD: AriAnnaPress, 1987.

Greenspan, Stanley. *First Feelings*. New York: Viking Penguin, Inc., 1985.

Gross, Harriet E. "Considering 'A Biosocial Perspective on Parenting.'" *Signs: Journal of Women on Culture and Society*, Vol. 4 No. 4, University of Chicago, 1979.

Guarendi, Ray, and David Eich. *Back to the Family*. New York: Simon and Schuster, 1991.

Harvey, Gail, ed. *A Mother Is Love*. New York: Gramercy Books, 1992.

Hallowell, Christopher. *Father to the Man*. New York: William Morrow and Company, 1987.

Institute for American Values. *Family Affairs*, Vol. 4 No. 1/2, Winter/Spring 1991.

Institute for American Values. *The Family in America*, Vol. 2 No. 8, August 1988.

Jackson, Deborah. *Three in a Bed*. New York: Avon Books, 1989.

Jefferson, B.G., and J.L. Nichols. *Safe Counsel*. Chicago: Franklin Publishing Company, 1928.

Josselyn, Irene M. *Psychological Development of Children*. New York: Family Service Association of America, 1967.

Kagan, J. "Cross-Cultural Perspectives on Early Development." *American Psychologist*, No. 28, 1973.

Kaminer, Wendy. *I'm Dysfunctional, You're Dysfunctional*. New York: Addison-Wesley Publishing Company, 1992.

Kennell, John, and Mary E. Bergen. "Early Childhood Separation." *Pediatrics*, No. 37, 1966.

Kippley, Sheila. *Breastfeeding and Natural Child Spacing*. Cincinnati, OH: Couple to Couple League, 1974.

Kitzinger, Sheila. *Women As Mothers*. New York: First Vintage Books, September 1980.

Klaus, Marshall H., and John H. Kennell. *Maternal-Infant Bonding*. St. Louis: C.V. Mosby Company, 1976.

Kramer, Rita. *In Defense of the Family*. New York: Basic Books, 1983.

Lakoff, Robin. *Talking Power*. New York: Basic Books, 1990.

Lansky, Vicki. *The Best of Practical Parenting*. Deephaven, MN: Book Peddlers of Deephaven, 1987.

Leach, Penelope. *Your Baby and Child From Birth to Age Five*. New York: Alfred A. Knopf, Inc., 1989.

LeShan, Eda. *When Your Child Drives You Crazy*. New York: St. Martin's Paperbacks, 1986.

Lewin, Miriam, ed. *In the Shadow of the Past: Psychology Portrays the Sexes*. New York: Columbia University Press, 1984.

Liedloff, Jean. *The Continuum Concept*. Reading, MA: Addison-Wesley Publishing Group, 1985.

Littner, Ner. *Custody and Visitation Arrangements*. Franklin Park, IL: La Leche League International.

Logan, Julie, and Arthur Howard. *The World According to He and She*. New York: Dell Publishing, 1992.

Luks, Allan, and Peggy Payne. *The Healing Power of Doing Good*. New York: Fawcett Columbia Books, 1991.

Macky, Wade. "Parameters of the Adult-Male Child." *Ethology and Sociobiology*, 1:59-76 1979, Elsevier North Holland Inc., 1979.

Madansky, Deborah, and Craig Edelbrock. "Cosleeping in a Community Sample of 2- and 3-year old Children." *Pediatrics*, Vol. 86 No. 2, August 1990.

May, Robert. *Sex and Fantasy*. New York: W.W. Norton and Company, 1980.

McClure, Vimala. *The Tao of Motherhood*. Willow Spring, MO: Nucleus Publishers, 1991.

McGee-Cooper, Ann. *Building Brain Power*. Dallas, TX: By the author, 1982.

McKenna, James. *An Anthropological Perspective on the SIDS*. Manuscript, Department of Sociology, Pomona College, Pomona, CA, 1987.

McKenna, James. "Researching the Sudden Infant Death Syndrome (SIDS): The Role of Ideology in Biomedical Sciences." Monograph Series of the New Liberal Arts Program. Stony

Brook, NY: Research Foundation of the State University of New York, 1991.

McKenna, James. "SIDS Research." *Mothering*, Winter 1992.

Mead, Margaret. *Letters From the Field: 1925-1975*. New York: Harper and Row, 1977.

Moir, Anne, and David Jessel. *Brain Sex*. New York: Lyle Stewart, 1991.

Montagu, Ashley. *Touching*. New York: Columbia University Press, 1971.

Newton, Niles. *Newton on Birth and Women*. Seattle, WA: Birth and Life Bookstore, 1990.

Ohess, Stella, and Jean Whitebread. *Daughters*. New York: Doubleday, 1978.

Osherson, Samuel. *Finding Our Fathers*. New York: Fawcett Columbine, 1986.

Pearce, Joseph C. *Magical Child Matures*. New York: E.P. Dutton, Inc., 1985.

Peck, M. Scott. *The Road Less Traveled*. New York: Simon and Schuster, 1978.

Piaget, Jean. *The Psychology of the Child*. New York: Basic Books, 1969.

Pomeranz, Virginia F. *The First Five Years*. New York: St. Martin's Press, 1984.

Postman, Neil. *The Disappearance of Childhood*. New York: Delacorte Press, 1982.

Quotes and *Comments on Mother/Baby Separation*. Franklin Park, IL: La Leche League International.

Quinn, Sally. "The Feminist Betrayal." *Reader's Digest*, June 1992.

Reich, Hanns. *Children and Their Mothers*. New York: Hill and Wang, 1964.

Richards, Martin, ed. *The Integration of a Child Into a Social World*. London: Cambridge University Press, 1974.

Riordan, Jan, and Kathleen G. Auerbach. *Breastfeeding and Human Lactation*. Boston: Jones and Bartlett, 1993.

Rodgers, Joann Ellison, and Michael F. Cataldo. *Raising Sons.* New York: New American Library, 1984.

Rogers, Katherine, and William McCarthy, eds. *The Meridian Anthology of Early Women Writers.* New York: NAL Penguin, 1987.

Rossi, Alice. "A Biosocial Perspective on Parenting." *Daedalus,* Spring 1977.

Rossi, Alice. "The Family." *Daedalus,* Spring 1977.

Ryerson, Alice Judson. "Medical Advice on Childrearing 1550-1990." *Harvard Educational Review* 31:302, 1961.

Sammons, William H.A. *The Self-Calmed Baby.* Boston: Little, Brown and Company, 1989.

Sanford, John A., and George Lough. *What Men Are Like.* New York: Paulist Press, 1988.

Sanger, Sirgay, and John Kelly. *You and Your Baby's First Year.* New York: Bantam Books, 1987.

Salk, Lee. *What Every Child Would Like His Parents to Know.* New York: David McKay Company, 1972.

Schmitt, Barton D. *Your Child's Health.* New York: Bantam Books, 1987.

Sears, William. *Becoming a Father.* Franklin Park, IL: La Leche League International, 1986.

Sears, William. *Creative Parenting.* New York, Dodd, Mead & Company, 1987.

Sege, Irene. "Fathers Called Crucial to Families." *The Boston Globe,* 10 January 1992.

Shagnon, Napoleon A. *Yanomamo: The Last Days of Eden.* New York: Harcourt Brace Jovanovich, 1992.

Shiff, Eileen, ed. *Experts Advise Parents.* New York: Bantam Doubleday Dell Publishing Group, 1987.

Sivertson, Howard. "A Family Tradition." *Once Upon an Isle.* Mount Horeb, WI: Wisconsin Folk Museum, 1992.

Smalley, Gary, and John Trent. *The Language of Love.* Pomona, CA: Focus on Family Publishing, 1988.

Smith, Huston. *The Religions of Man*. New York: Harper and Row, 1991.

Sowell, Thomas. "The Big Lie." *Forbes*, 23 December 1991.

Spock, Benjamin. *Baby and Child Care*. New York: Pocket Books, 1971.

Spock, Benjamin. *Dr. Spock on Parenting*. New York: Simon and Schuster, 1988.

Stephen Hawking's A Brief History of Time: A Reader's Companion, ed. S. Hawking, prepared by Gene Stone. New York: Bantam Books, 1992.

Swigart, Jane. *The Myth of the Bad Mother*. New York: Doubleday, 1991.

Tannen, Deborah. *You Just Don't Understand: Women and Men in Conversation*. New York: William Morrow and Company, 1990.

Taubman, Bruce. *Curing Infant Colic*. New York: Bantam Books, 1990.

"Teaching Baby to Sleep Through the Night." *Psychology Today*, April 1989.

Theroux, Phyllis. *Night Lights*. New York: Viking Penguin, 1987.

Thevenin, Tine. *Luck Is Not a Butterfly*. Bloomington, MN: By the author, 1988.

Tobey, Susan B. *Art of Motherhood*. New York: Abbeville Press Publishers, 1991.

Toufexis, Anafasia. "Coming From a Different Place." *Time*, Special Women's Issue, Fall 1990.

Towle, A. *Fathers*. New York: Simon and Schuster, 1986.

Uhlenbuth, Karen. "Life Without Father." *Kansas City Star*, February 23, 1992.

"Unite and Conquer," *Newsweek*, 5 February 1990.

Verny, Thomas, and Pamela Weintraub. *Nurturing the Unborn Child*. New York: Dell Publishing, 1991.

Virden, Susan Flagler. "The Relationship Between Infant Feeding Method and Maternal Role Adjustment." *Journal of Nurse Midwifery*, Vol. 33 No. 1, January 1988.

Weiner, Bernard. "Initiating Our Teenage Sons." *Mothering*, No. 67, Summer 1993.

White, Burton L. *The First Three Years of Life*. Englewood Cliffs, NJ: Prentice-Hall, 1975.

Whiting, John M. "22 Effects of Climate on Certain Cultural Practices." *Explorations in Cultural Anthropology*, ed. W.H. Goodenough. New York: McGraw-Hill, 1964.

Whiting, John. "Environmental Constraints on Infant Care Practices." *Handbook of Cross-Cultural Human Development*, ed. Robert Monroe, Ruth Monroe, and Beatrice Whiting. New York: Garland STPN Press, 1981.

Whitman, Walt. *Leaves of Grass*. New York: Viking Press, 1945.

Wilson-Clay, Barbara. "Extended Breast-Feeding as a Legal Issue: An Annotated Bibliography." *Journal of Human Lactation*, 6(2), 1990.

The Womanly Art of Breastfeeding. Franklin Park, IL: La Leche League International, 1991.

Wrigley, Elizabeth, and Sally Hutchinson. "Long-Term Breast feeding: The Secret Bond." *Journal of Nurse-Midwifery*, Vol. 35 No. 1, January/February 1990.

Recommended Reading

GENDER DIFFERENCES

Cris Evatt, *He and She*, Conari Press.

Carol Gilligan, *In a Different Voice*, Harvard University Press.

Anne Moir and David Jessel, *Brain Sex*, Lyle Stewart.

Deborah Tannen, Ph.D, *That's Not What I Meant! How Conversational Style Makes or Breaks Your Relations With Others*, Ballantine Books.

Deborah Tannen, Ph.D, *You Just Don't Understand: Women and Men in Conversation*, William Morrow and Company, Inc.

PARENTING

Anything by Dr. Louise Bates Ames.

Family Affairs, a newsletter published by the Institute for American Values, New York, NY.

Anything by Dr. Penelope Leach.

Jean Liedloff, *The Continuum Concept,* Addison-Wesley Publishing Group.

William Sears, *Becoming a Father*, La Leche League International.

Jerrold Lee Shapiro, *The Measure of a Man*, Delacorte Press.

The Womanly Art of Breastfeeding. La Leche League International.

Index

Separation anxiety, 61
Shiff, Eileen, 88
Shunning, 110
SIDS. *See* Sudden infant death
    syndrome.
Simultaneous multiple
    involvements, 126
Siriano people, 106
Sivertson, Howard, 151
Sleep problems, 63
Sleeping arrangements
    breast-feeding and, 63
    child spacing and, 115
    independence and, 62–65
    men's and women's attitudes
        toward, 62–63, 65
    as source of conflict, 14, 41
    sudden infant death syn-
        drome and, 64–65, 115–
        116
    traditional child-rearing
        practices and, 74, 104
Smith, Huston, 128
Smith, Lendon H., 85
Southern California Psycho-
    analytic Institute, 101
Sowell, Thomas, 153–154
Spock, Benjamin, 9, 84, 85,
    98–99
Stanford, John, 44
Stress, 108, 145–146
    effect on children, 67, 69–70,
        109
    effect on mothers, 94–95
    men's and women's respon-
        ses to, 122, 123, 126
Sudden infant death
    syndrome, 64–65, 115–116,
    127
Sullivan, Louis W., 154
Support, 147–149. *See also*
    Emotional support.
Sweden, 73, 167

Talk. *See* Communication.
Talking Power, 86

Tannen, Deborah, 17, 18, 20,
    27–28, 38, 40, 100
Tension, release of. *See* Motion.
Thackeray, William Make-
    peace, 117
Three in a Bed, 111
Time, 18
Time-out, 91–92
Tobey, Susan B., 108
Toilet training, 104–105
Touching, 112. *See also*
    Holding.
*Touching: The Human Signi-
    ficance of the Skin*, 112
Toys. *See* Games and toys.
Traditional child-rearing
    practices. *See* Child
    rearing, traditional
    practices.
Training, 100–101
Transition period, 74, 78, 79,
    80, 121. *See also* Indepen-
    dence, development of.
*Treatise on the Physical and
    Medical Treatment of
    Children, A*, 3
Trust, 9, 66–67, 101–102, 112,
    126–127, 149, 150, 156, 157,
    160

UNICEF, 134
United States Children's
    Bureau, 52
University of California, 65
University of Chicago, 110
University of Kansas, 155
University of Massachusetts
    Medical School, 63
University of Michigan
    Medical Center, 61
University of Missouri, 154

Violence, 46, 153
Voth, Harold M., 112, 147–148

Wallerstein, Judith, 156

About the Author

Tine Thevenin was born in the Netherlands and was educated there and in the United States. She was a professional musician and teacher before becoming a mother, La Leche League counselor, and author of *The Family Bed: An Age Old Concept in Child Rearing*. That book has since sold over 100,000 copies, and was instrumental in reversing a decision in a criminal child abuse case in Massachusetts in 1987.

Mrs. Thevenin is also an accomplished triathlete, small business owner, and public speaker. She is vitally interested in health, and is actively involved in local and global environmental issues. Above all, Mrs. Thevenin feels that her role as mother has been the most important vocation in her life. She lives with her husband in Bloomington, Minnesota.